By Grace Are We Saved

By Grace Are We Saved

Robert L. Millet

BOOKCRAFT
Salt Lake City, Utah

Library of Congress Catalog Card Number: 89-61156

ISBN 0-88494-694-0

First Printing, 1989

Printed in the United States of America

Contents

Preface

It seems that whenever the subject of being saved by grace surfaces, many Latter-day Saints become defensive and eagerly move to one of two conclusions: (1) the word *salvation* refers only to resurrection, to deliverance from the grave; or (2) exaltation or eternal life is something which must be wholly merited or *earned*. This book has been written to address the issue of salvation by grace; essentially, I have concluded that both responses (above) are not only unnecessary and theologically misleading but also are potentially damaging to our spiritual well-being.

This topic—salvation by the grace of Christ—has weighed on my mind for many years. I have come to believe that our understanding and acceptance of the proper roles of the grace of God and the works of man can do much to draw us closer to him who is described in scripture as being "full of grace and truth." In addition, a proper perspective on what the Lord has done and continues to do for us can go a long way toward reducing much of the anxiety and discouragement of members of the Church who wrestle constantly with what they view as a huge chasm between the ideal—the divinely given standard of perfection—and their own state, which is fraught with human weaknesses and limitations.

This work is not an official publication of The Church of Jesus Christ of Latter-day Saints or of Brigham Young University. Though I have sought in my writing to be in harmony with the holy scriptures and the teachings of the latter-day Apostles and prophets, the book is a private endeavor, and the conclusions drawn from the evidence cited are my own. I do, however, believe them to be true.

Special thanks are due to Joell Woodbrey, a capable and conscientious secretary and assistant. She has enthusiastically read the chapters one by one and offered helpful and meaningful suggestions in both content and organization. I am indebted to Robert J. Matthews, my colleague and mentor and the dean of Religious Education at Brigham Young University, who has offered both example and encouragement for this and many other projects. Finally, I owe a special debt of gratitude and love to my wife, Shauna, who has stood by me, sustained me, and encouraged my research and writing. Without her proddings and suggestions, so many things essential to this book would not have materialized or even mattered.

Preparing each of the chapters which follows has proven to be a rigorous but reverential undertaking. The study, pondering, and prayer that have been necessary preparation for the organization and writing have taxed me to the limit, both physically and spiritually. These labors have been matched only by an ever-expanding love of the Lord and a sense of awe and wonder in contemplating his gifts and graces, an experience which necessarily follows from repeated and intense reflection upon this subject. My soul has come to resonate with the words of Jacob: "Cheer up your hearts, and remember that ye are free to act for yourselves—to choose the way of everlasting death or the way of eternal life. Wherefore, my beloved brethren, reconcile yourselves to the will of God, and not to the will of the devil and the flesh; and remember, after ye are reconciled unto God, that it is only in and through the grace of God that ye are saved." (2 Nephi 10:23-24.)

Introduction

Some years ago I sat with my counselors in a bishopric meeting. The session was drawing to a close because sacrament
meeting would be starting in just ten minutes. A knock came
at the door as we were making our way out of the office into
the foyer. A young woman from my ward was there, who
asked if she could visit with me for a moment. I indicated to
her that we could chat for a bit, but that sacrament meeting
would be starting soon. She assured me that we would be together for only a minute or two.

After we had been seated for a few seconds, she said:
"Bishop, I need to confess a sin."

I was startled with the suddenness of the statement, but,
managing to hold my composure, I offered the following:
"Well, that could take some time, couldn't it? Shall we meet
after the block of meetings today?"

She quickly responded: "Oh no! This will just take a second."

I nodded and asked her to go ahead, and she proceeded to
describe in some detail a very serious moral transgression in

which she had been involved. It was now about one minute before the meetings were to start, and so I tried again: "Why don't we get together after priesthood and Relief Society meetings."

She then staggered me with, "Well, I don't know why we would need to, unless it would be helpful to you, or something."

I indicated that such a meeting might prove beneficial to both of us. She agreed to return.

Three hours later, and after we had exchanged a few pleasantries, I asked her, "How do you feel about what has happened?"

She responded, "Just fine." I must have shown my perplexity, because she added: "For a number of hours I felt bad about what had happened, but it's okay now because I've repented."

I couldn't ask her the question fast enough, "What do you mean when you say that you have repented?" (She had explained to me earlier that the transgression had taken place on Friday night, and it was now Sunday afternoon.)

At that point, she reached into her purse, rearranged a few items, and retrieved a yellow sheet of legal-size paper. Pointing one by one to various headings that began with *R*, she said, "I've done this, and this, and this, and this, and finally I've confessed to you. I've repented."

"It seems to me that you've skipped an *R*, that your list is missing something," I said.

A startled but persistent look was in her eyes, and I noted a slight impatience with me as she said, "No, that can't be. I have everything listed here!"

"The *R* you're missing," I responded, "is *Redeemer*. You have no place for Christ on your list. I mean, what does Jesus Christ have to do with your transgression? What does what happened in Gethsemane and on Calvary some two thousand years ago have to do with what happened to you two nights ago?"

She answered: "Jesus died for me. He died for my sins."

To almost every question I asked thereafter about the Atonement she gave a perfect answer—at least, a perfectly correct answer. She had been well trained, and her answers reflected an awareness of the doctrines associated with repentance. But the answers were all totally cerebral, straight from memory and mind—not from the heart. She obviously saw no real tie between her own ungodly actions and the infinite actions of a God. We spent several hours together that day and many days thereafter—searching the scriptures, praying together, and counseling over the way back to the strait and narrow path. We talked often and intently about Jesus Christ. She came in time to know the correct answers—this time by feeling, that is, from the heart.

I have never been quite the same since that experience. Nor, I must add, was this the only one of its kind that I have had. Again and again I find members of the Church uncertain and aimless in their search for spiritual rest, unsure of the way to peace and happiness after serious sin. Often, very often, they, like my young ward member, have not made the vital connection between what Jesus the Christ has done for us and what we can and must now do. Such occasions as these have motivated me to search carefully the scriptures and the words of the modern prophets, to turn my heart to the Lord and seek in prayer to know and understand better finite man's relationship to an infinite Redeemer. As a result I have come to believe more strongly every day in the testimony of Nephi and have taken his words as counsel and warning for those of us who must live in a cynical and secular world, in a world which promises formulas and keys and ready access and quick-fixes: "We talk of Christ," he observed, "we rejoice in Christ, we preach of Christ, we prophesy of Christ, and we write according to our prophecies, that our children may know to what source they may look for a remission of their sins" (2 Nephi 25:26).

My search of the scriptures has led me to an even deeper appreciation for our Lord and for what he has done for mankind. It has also caused me to appreciate the marvelous flood of light and intelligence that has come to us through Joseph Smith, the Book of Mormon, and modern revelation, assorted gems of priceless value which lay appropriate stress upon the grace of the Savior, Jesus Christ, and on the concurrent obe-

dience and faithfulness required of those who claim kinship
and discipleship with him. It would seem to me that men and
women could fall into at least two theological traps in this
regard: (1) either they could come to believe in salvation by
grace alone and hence in the irrelevance of one's obedience
and works, or (2) they could come to trust wholly in their own
labors and genius, erroneously supposing that what they
merit hereafter is a product solely of what they achieve or accomplish on their own here.

Perhaps one of the finest statements in all of our literature
concerning the proper role of grace and works is contained in
the Dictionary of the LDS Edition of the King James Bible, in
which the word *grace* is defined as "a word that occurs frequently in the New Testament, especially in the writings of
Paul. The main idea of the word is divine means of help or
strength, given through the bounteous mercy and love of
Jesus Christ." The article continues:

> It is through the grace of the Lord Jesus, made pos-
> sible by his atoning sacrifice, that mankind will be
> raised in immortality, every person receiving his body
> from the grave in a condition of everlasting life. It is
> likewise through the grace of the Lord that individuals,
> through faith in the atonement of Jesus Christ and re-
> pentance of their sins, receive strength and assistance to
> do good works that they otherwise would not be able to
> maintain if left to their own means.
>
> This grace is an enabling power that allows men and
> women to lay hold on eternal life and exaltation after
> they have expended their own best efforts.
>
> Divine grace is needed by every soul in consequence
> of the fall of Adam and also because of man's weak-
> nesses and shortcomings. However, grace cannot suffice
> without total effort on the part of the recipient. Hence
> the explanation, "It is by grace that we are saved, after
> all we can do" (2 Nephi 25:23). It is truly the grace of
> Jesus Christ that makes salvation possible. (P. 697.)

As with so many others, "I stand all amazed at the love
Jesus offers me, confused at the grace that so fully he proffers

me" (*Hymns*, 1985, No. 193). I have no hesitation and feel no shame in acknowledging that I do not understand the particulars of how the atonement of Christ was brought to pass, how it was that Jesus of Nazareth assumed the burden of the sins of mankind. I do know, however, that it has been accomplished, and that even though for the time being it is inexplicable to finite minds, we can take full advantage of the graces and gifts of God so readily available through him who is mighty to save.

I know that because of the tender regard and selfless sacrifice of that one being, "unto every one of us is given grace according to the measure of the gift of Christ" (Ephesians 4:7). Like Nephi, "I glory in [this] truth. I glory in my Jesus, for he hath redeemed my soul from hell" (2 Nephi 33:6). "For the grace of God which bringeth salvation to all men, hath appeared; teaching us that, denying ungodliness and worldly lusts, we should live soberly, righteously, and godly, in this present world; looking for that blessed hope, and the glorious appearing of the great God and our Savior Jesus Christ; who gave himself for us, that he might redeem us from all iniquity, and purify unto himself a peculiar people, zealous of good works" (JST, Titus 2:11–14).

The way is prepared from the fall of man, and
salvation is free.

—2 Nephi 2:4

CHAPTER 1

Salvation Is Free

Salvation, which is exaltation, which is eternal life, is free. It
is not something for which we can barter, nor something
which may be purchased with money. Nor in the strictest
sense is it something which may be *earned*. More correctly,
salvation is a gift, a gift most precious, something gloriously
transcendent which may only be *inherited*. "If thou wilt do
good," the Lord explained to Oliver Cowdery, "yea, and hold
out faithful to the end, thou shalt be saved in the kingdom of
God, which is the greatest of all the gifts of God; for there is
no gift greater than the gift of salvation" (D&C 6:13). To
David Whitmer that same Lord affirmed: "If you keep my
commandments and endure to the end you shall have eternal
life, which gift is the greatest of all the gifts of God" (D&C
14:7; for a detailed discussion of the meaning of salvation see
Millet and McConkie, *The Life Beyond*, pp. 131–35).

In commending his son Jacob on the manner in which he
had learned wisdom and followed righteousness in his youth,
Lehi said: "Thou hast beheld in thy youth his [Christ's] glory;

wherefore, thou art blessed even as they unto whom he shall minister in the flesh; for the Spirit is the same, yesterday, today, and forever. And *the way is prepared from the fall of man, and salvation is free."* (2 Nephi 2:4, italics added.) Indeed, salvation is free, freely available, freely to be found by those who seek and inquire and obey. When the prophets who lived before the coming of our Lord in the flesh spoke of salvation being free, they were in effect declaring the same doctrine which would flow from the lips and pens of Apostles and prophets in the statement that we are saved by the grace of Christ. That is to say, free salvation is salvation by grace.

"The questions then are: What salvation is free? What salvation comes by the grace of God? With all the emphasis of the rolling thunders of Sinai, we answer: All salvation is free; all comes by the merits and mercy and grace of the Holy Messiah; there is no salvation of any kind, nature, or degree that is not bound to Christ and his atonement." (Bruce R. McConkie, *The Promised Messiah*, pp. 346–47.) In the words of Isaiah and Nephi, the people of the earth are summoned to come to the waters of life, to acquire the milk and honey of the gospel, but to do so without money and without price. "Hath [the Lord] commanded any that they should not partake of his salvation?" Nephi asked. "Nay," he answered, "but he hath given it free for all men. . . . Behold, hath the Lord commanded any that they should not partake of his goodness? Behold I say unto you, Nay; but all men are privileged the one like unto the other, and none are forbidden." (2 Nephi 26:25–28.)

A Gospel of Grace

In our efforts to stress the importance of good works—of receiving the ordinances of salvation, of living by every word of God, of standing as witnesses of Christ at all times, and of involving ourselves in the acts of Christian service that always characterize the disciples of Jesus in any age—we are sometimes wont to overlook the simple yet profound reality that the plan of salvation, the gospel of Jesus Christ, is truly a gospel of grace. "Does salvation come by grace, by grace alone," Elder Bruce R. McConkie asked, "by grace without works? It surely does," he answered, "without any question, in all its parts, types, kinds, and degrees."

We are saved by grace, without works; it is a gift of God. How else could it come?

In his goodness and grace the great God ordained and established the plan of salvation. No works on our part were required.

In his goodness and grace he created this earth and all that is on it, with man as the crowning creature of his creating—without which creation his spirit children could not obtain immortality and eternal life. No works on our part were required.

In his goodness and grace he provided for the Fall of man, thus bringing mortality and death and a probationary estate into being—without all of which there would be no immortality and eternal life. And again no works on our part were required.

In his goodness and grace—and this above all—he gave his Only Begotten Son to ransom man and all life from the temporal and spiritual death brought into the world by the Fall of Adam. . . .

There is nothing any man could do to create himself. This was the work of the Lord God.

Nor did we have any part in the Fall of man, without which there could be no salvation. The Lord provided the way, and Adam and Eve put the system into operation.

And finally, there neither has been, nor is, nor ever can be any way nor means by which man alone can, by any power he possesses, redeem himself. ("What Think Ye of Salvation by Grace?" p. 47.)

More specifically, through the atonement of Christ there are numerous blessings which accrue to mortal man, these coming as unconditional benefits of the work of redemption, acts of pure grace.

Had there been no atonement, because of the fall of our first parents this earth and all forms of life upon it would have been shut out forever from the presence of the Eternal God; man would have been severed completely from the regenerating powers of the Spirit. But because of the love and condescensions and mercies of the Holy One, the light and life of Christ are extended to earth and its inhabitants, "otherwise [we] could not abound" (D&C 88:49–50; compare 11:28; 39:1–3; Mosiah 2:21).

Second, agency and moral freedom are made available to all through the Atonement. "The Messiah cometh in the fulness of time," Lehi taught, "that he may redeem the children of men from the fall. And because that they are redeemed from the fall they have become free forever, knowing good from evil; to act for themselves and not to be acted upon. . . . They are free to choose liberty and eternal life, through the great Mediator of all men, or to choose captivity and death, according to the captivity and power of the devil." (2 Nephi 2:26–27; compare 10:23; Helaman 14:30.) People in all ages are thus able to stand fast "in the liberty wherewith Christ hath made us free" (Galatians 5:1).

Third, those who live and die without gospel law or without understanding or accountability are not subject to the demands of God's justice. Jacob explained therefore that in cases "where there is no condemnation, the mercies of the Holy One of Israel have claim upon them, because of the atonement" (2 Nephi 9:25–26). Benjamin likewise taught his people that the blood of Christ atones "for the sins of those who have fallen by the transgression of Adam, who have died not knowing the will of God concerning them, or who have ignorantly sinned" (Mosiah 3:11; compare 15:24; Moroni 8:22). This principle and benefit applies to little children who die before the time of accountability: they remain innocent before the Lord and are not subject to the tempter's power; they are assured of eternal life (see Moses 6:53–54; Moroni 8; D&C 29:46–48; 93:38–42).

Finally, because of the ransoming power and the intercessory role of Jesus Christ, all men and women will follow the pattern of their Risen Lord as to the resurrection: they will receive the free gift of immortality—they will be raised from the dead in the resurrection to inherit a physical body. "For since by man came death, by man came also the resurrection of the dead. For as in Adam all die, even so in Christ shall all be made alive." (1 Corinthians 15:21–22.) When the time has fully come and the trump is sounded, "then shall all the dead awake, for their graves shall be opened, and they shall come forth—yea, even all" (D&C 29:26; compare Alma 11:40–44). No works or labors or mortal deeds are necessary to bring these eventualities to pass; they come from a gracious Lord who desires to save all of the children of the Father.

Truly we are the recipients of graces without number, are beneficiaries of the Lord's love and condescensions, of gifts which are beyond our power to work for, earn, or even adequately express gratitude for. As we shall see presently, in order to gain eternal life men and women must demonstrate, through faithful living, a genuine receipt of the Atonement and the plan of salvation: they must keep the commandments and evidence their fidelity and devotion to the Lord and his work in order to accept these precious gifts. "If we walk in the light, as he is in the light, we have fellowship one with another, and the blood of Jesus Christ his Son cleanseth us from all sin" (1 John 1:7). But such works of man, no matter what their quantity or quality, in no way alter the fact that we are saved by the grace of Christ—by and through unearned divine assistance. Like Nephi, we joy in the covenants of the Lord, we delight "in his grace, and in his justice, and power, and mercy in the great and eternal plan of deliverance from death" (2 Nephi 11:5).

All have sinned, and come short of the glory of God.

—Romans 3:23

CHAPTER 2

"For All Have Sinned . . ."

Adam's fall brought death into the world. Because of the nature of this fallen state, men are alienated from things of righteousness; they are without God in the world, and most of earth's inhabitants choose to walk in broad and forbidden paths—they go contrary to the things of God and thus contrary to the nature of happiness (Alma 41:10–11). They become natural men, enemies to God and thus enemies to their own best interests (Mosiah 2:36–37; 3:19).

During a long day of debate with his opponents, Jesus delivered the following parable: "A certain man had two sons; and he came to the first, and said, Son, go work to day in my vineyard. He [the son] answered and said, I will not: but afterward he repented, and went. And he came to the second, and said likewise. And he answered and said, I go, sir: and went not. Whether of them twain did the will of his father?" (Matthew 21:28–31.) One "may wonder why this story does not include a third son who said, 'I will,' and kept his word. Perhaps it is because this story characterizes humanity, and we all fall short (cf. Romans 3:23). Thus Jesus could describe only two kinds of religious people: those who pretend to be obedient but are actually rebels, and those who begin as rebels but repent." (Taken from *The Gospel According to Jesus* by John MacArthur, Jr., p. 167. Copyright © 1988 by John F. MacArthur. Used by permission of Zondervan Publishing House.)

Latter-day Saints reject the false notion so prevalent in Christendom that men are by nature depraved creatures, unable to even choose the right. We "believe that men will be punished for their own sins, and not for Adam's transgression" (Articles of Faith 1:2), meaning, of course, that we reject the heinous idea that an "original sin" entailed upon the posterity of our first parents a taint and a stain transmitted through birth. The Augustinian concept of man as a wormish and vile thing is foreign to the truth and counterproductive to the plan of the Father. At the same time, the scriptures clearly attest that as a result of the events in Eden men and women are fallen and lost, subject to the whims and pulls of the flesh. All things would have so remained had there been no atonement.

One of the most important realizations any person can have is coming face to face with his or her mortality, becoming painfully aware of his or her weakness and infirmities. It is only as we sense our inadequacies, as we admit our own human limitations, that we eagerly turn to him who offers deliverance and relief from the weighty burden of sin. Jesus said to the self-righteous Pharisees of his day: "If ye were blind, ye should have no sin: but now ye say, We see; therefore your sin remaineth" (John 9:41). Jacob made very clear the fact that "whoso knocketh, to him will [the Lord] open; and the wise, and the learned, and they that are rich, who are puffed up because of their learning, and their wisdom, and their riches—yea, they are they whom he despiseth; and save they shall cast these things away, and consider themselves fools before God, and come down in the depths of humility, he will not open unto them. But the things of the wise and the prudent shall be hid from them forever—yea, that happiness which is prepared for the saints." (2 Nephi 9:42–43.)

Only those who know their needs will have them met and satisfied. Only those who hunger and thirst after righteousness can be filled with the Holy Ghost. Because all have sinned and come short of the glory of God (Romans 3:23), "Jesus entered this world on a search-and-rescue mission for sinners. That truth is what characterizes the gospel as good news." (MacArthur, *The Gospel According to Jesus*, p. 90. See copyright detail, p. 14.)

Part of recognizing one's humanity is recognizing that sins are more than mistakes, more than accidents; when persisted in, they bring us into rebellion against God and all that is good. In describing the need for and the process of repentance, the great Christian thinker C. S. Lewis observed that fallen man has "tried to set up on his own, to behave as if he belonged to himself. In other words, fallen man is not simply an imperfect creature who needs improvement: he is a rebel who must lay down his arms. Laying down your arms, surrendering, saying you are sorry, realising that you have been on the wrong track and getting ready to start life over again from the ground floor—that is the only way out of a 'hole.' This process of surrender—this movement full-speed astern—is what Christians call repentance." (Taken from *Mere Christianity* by C. S. Lewis, p. 59, Macmillan Publishing Company, 1960. Copyright © by William Collins & Sons.)

After King Benjamin had given an account of his reign and ministry, after he had answered with a clear conscience to his people concerning his service to men and God, he pleaded as follows: "And behold also, if I, whom ye call your king, who has spent his days in your service, and yet has been in the service of God, do merit any thanks from you, O how you ought to thank your heavenly King!"

> I say unto you, my brethren, that if you should render all the thanks and praise which your whole soul has power to possess, to that God who has created you, and has kept and preserved you, and has caused that ye should rejoice, and has granted that ye should live in peace one with another—
>
> I say unto you that if ye should serve him who has created you from the beginning, and is preserving you from day to day, by lending you breath, that ye may live and move and do according to your own will, and

even supporting you from one moment to another—I
say, if ye should serve him with all your whole souls yet
ye would be unprofitable servants. (Mosiah 2:19–21.)

Later Benjamin would invite his people to ponder upon "the
greatness of God, and your own nothingness, and his goodness and long-suffering towards you, unworthy creatures"
(Mosiah 4:11). The Lord owes no man or woman. He not only
rewards his children for all their righteous deeds (see Mosiah
2:22–24), but he always overpays. So often the blessings of
heaven reflect not man's goodness but God's.

After Moses had been transfigured, lifted spiritually to a
higher plane for a time, "the presence of God withdrew from
Moses, that his glory was not upon Moses; and Moses was
left unto himself. And as he was left unto himself, he fell unto
the earth. And it came to pass that it was for the space of
many hours before Moses did again receive his natural
strength like unto man; and he said unto himself: Now, for
this cause I know that man is nothing, which thing I never
had supposed." (Moses 1:9–10.) Truly, when compared with
the omnipotent majesty of God, man is nothing. Further,
without the refining and regenerating powers of the Spirit
which come from God, man is nothing. He is, without sacred
support, lower than the dust of the earth, for even the dust of
the earth obeys the commands of higher powers (see Mosiah
2:25; 4:2–8; Helaman 12:7–8).

Man has no power to transform a fallen soul. Indeed, to renew the mind and heart of man is the work of one greater
than man, the work of a God. Paul, speaking for all men and
women, said: "For I know that in me, that is, in my flesh,
dwelleth no good thing; for to will is present with me, but to
perform that which is good I find not, only in Christ." (JST,
Romans 7:19.)

The grace of God is available to all. But only those who
come to realize their spiritual bankruptcy—who recognize the
wide chasm between their own labors and the perfections of
Deity, and who resolve to draw upon the infinite powers of
him who is mighty to save—only these grow in those spiritual

graces which lead to life eternal, for the Lord "scorneth the scorners: but he giveth grace unto the lowly" (Proverbs 3:34). That is to say, "God resisteth the proud, but giveth grace unto the humble" (James 4:6; 1 Peter 5:5).

Too often people trust "in themselves that they [are] righteous." Jesus warned of such things. "Two men went up into the temple to pray," he taught; "the one a Pharisee, and the other a publican," a tax gatherer. "The Pharisee stood and prayed thus *with himself*, God, I thank thee, that I am not as other men are, extortioners, unjust, adulterers, or even as this publican." And then the Pharisee extolled his own virtues: "I fast twice in the week, I give tithes of all that I possess. And the publican, standing afar off, would not lift up so much as his eyes unto heaven"—recognizing his unworthiness before an all-seeing and perfect God—"but smote upon his breast, saying, God be merciful to me a sinner." The Lord reads the hearts of men and knows their desires. He discerns duplicity and perceives perversion. He rewards those who acknowledge their weakness and trust in his strength. "I tell you," Jesus said, "this man [the publican] went down to his house justified rather than the other: for every one that exalteth himself shall be abased; and he that humbleth himself shall be exalted." (Luke 18:9-14, italics added.)

One of the marvelous insights provided by King Benjamin in the Book of Mormon is the knowledge that one may retain a remission of sins from day to day only through a humble recognition of one's limitations and a gracious acceptance of the Lord God's willingness to lift and lighten.

As ye have come to the knowledge of the glory of God, or if ye have known of his goodness and have tasted of his love, and have received a remission of your sins, which causeth such exceedingly great joy in your souls, even so I would that ye should *remember, and always retain in remembrance, the greatness of God, and your own nothingness,* and his goodness and long-suffering towards you, unworthy creatures, and humble yourselves even in the depths of humility, calling on the name of the Lord daily, and standing steadfastly in the faith of that which is to come, which was spoken by the mouth of the angel.

And behold, I say unto you that if ye do this ye shall always rejoice, and be filled with the love of God, and *always retain a remission of your sins;* and ye shall grow in the knowledge of the glory of him that created you, or in the knowledge of that which is just and true. (Mosiah 4:11–12, italics added.)

Indeed, "the Lord God is a sun and shield: the Lord will give grace and glory: no good thing will he withhold from them that walk uprightly" (Psalm 84:11).

There is no flesh that can dwell in the presence of God, save it be through the merits, and mercy, and grace of the Holy Messiah.

—2 Nephi 2:8

CHAPTER 3

Relying Wholly upon His Merits

What mortal can snatch pride and selfishness, lust and lewdness from a natural man and create a clean heart in its place? Indeed, no man but the Man of Holiness and the Son of Man can do such things; these are works and wonders beyond the power of even the most spiritually mature Saints to do. Servants of the Lord can and do function at their Master's behest in administering the gospel to the children of men. Legal administrators—agents of the Lord—can and do represent their divine principal in leading lost souls back to the fold of the Good Shepherd. But the miracle of change, the miracle associated with the renovation and regeneration of fallen man, is the work of a God. The true Saints of God have come to know and rely upon that transcendent power.

Why Jesus Was the Savior

Lehi testifed to his son Jacob that "redemption cometh in and through the Holy Messiah; for he is full of grace and truth." He continued: "Wherefore, how great the importance to make these things known unto the inhabitants of the earth, that they may know that there is no flesh that can dwell in the presence of God, save it be through the merits, and mercy, and grace of the Holy Messiah, who layeth down his life according to the flesh, and taketh it again by the power of the Spirit, that he may bring to pass the resurrection of the dead, being the first that should rise." (2 Nephi 2:6, 8.)

A number of significant doctrinal points surface in this poignant passage. First, we note with interest that Lehi's stress is not upon the importance of man's works or merits— as essential as they may be—but rather on the merits and mercy and grace of Christ. It is through what the Savior has done, the works and merits of the Lord Jesus that no mortal man could accomplish, that salvation is made available. As we have already noted, had there been no atonement there would be no salvation of any type or kind or nature. Earlier in Lehi's counsel to his son, the aged patriarch-prophet said: "Wherefore, thy soul shall be blessed, and thou shalt dwell safely with thy brother, Nephi; and thy days shall be spent in the service of thy God. Wherefore, I know that thou art redeemed, because of the righteousness of thy Redeemer; for thou hast beheld that in the fulness of time he cometh to bring salvation unto men." (2 Nephi 2:3.)

Second, the prophets are bold in declaring that we are able to rely on Christ because of his sinless state, because he qualified in every sense for salvation through his own merits, through his own moral perfection. He "was in all points tempted like as we are, yet without sin" (Hebrews 4:15). Christ never took a backward step, never took a moral detour. He never knew—until the hours of atonement—the awful agony of alienation from things holy; he never experienced until Gethsemane and Calvary the loss of the Spirit of the Father, the loss that follows in the wake of willful sin. Being perfect, therefore, he was qualified, capable, and more than willing to help us who are so very imperfect.

Further, and perhaps more important, Jesus of Nazareth was literally the Son of the Almighty Elohim, and as such inherited from his exalted sire the powers of immortality, the ability to live forever. From his mother, the mortal Mary, he inherited mortality, the capacity to die. "Therefore doth my Father love me," Jesus stated, "because I lay down my life, that I might take it again. No man taketh it from me, but I lay it down of myself. I have power to lay it down, and I have power to take it again. This commandment have I received of my Father." (John 10:17–18.) Thus, in the language of Lehi, Christ laid down his life according to the flesh—he submitted to the universal commonality, death—and took it up again by the power of the Spirit: he rose from the tomb in glory by virtue of his inherited power over death. In describing the manner in which Jesus Christ was able to pay the "debt" incurred by man through the Fall and through individual sinfulness, C. S. Lewis has wisely observed:

> We are told that Christ was killed for us, that His death has washed out our sins, and that by dying he disabled death itself. That is the formula. That is Christianity. That is what has to be believed. Any theories we build up as to how Christ's death did all this are, in my view, quite secondary. . . . The [theory] most people have heard is the one . . . about our being let off because Christ had volunteered to bear a punishment instead of us. Now on the face of it that is a very silly theory. If God was prepared to let us off, why on earth did He not do so? And what possible point could there be in punishing an innocent person instead? None at all that I can see, if you are thinking of punishment in the police-court sense. On the other hand, if you think of a debt there is plenty of point in a person who has some assets paying it on behalf of someone who has not. Or if you take "paying the penalty," not in the sense of being punished, but in the more general sense of "standing the racket," or "footing the bill," then, of course, it is a matter of common experience that, when one person has got himself into a hole, the trouble of getting him out usually falls on a kind friend. . . .
>
> If I am drowning in a rapid river, a man who still has one foot on the bank may give me a hand which saves

my life. Ought I to shout back (between my gasps) "No,
it's not fair! You have an advantage! You're keeping
one foot on the bank"? That advantage—call it "unfair"
if you like—is the only reason why he can be of any use
to me. To what will you look for help if you will not
look to that which is stronger than yourself? (*Mere Christianity*, pp. 58–59, 61. See publishing detail, p. 15.)

Salvation Through His Merits Alone

It was in teaching the father of King Lamoni that Aaron,
the son of Mosiah, "did expound unto him the scriptures
from the creation of Adam, laying the fall of man before him,
and their carnal state and also the plan of redemption, which
was prepared from the foundation of the world, through
Christ, for all whosoever would believe on his name. And
since man had fallen he could not merit anything of himself;
but the sufferings and death of Christ atone for their sins,
through faith and repentance." (Alma 22:13–14.) Later in the
Book of Mormon story we read that Anti-Nephi-Lehi, the
brother of Lamoni and recent convert to the gospel path,
prayed: "I . . . thank my God, that by opening this corre-
spondence [that is, through the missionary labors of the sons
of Mosiah] we have been convinced of our sins, and of the
many murders which we have committed. And I also thank
my God, yea, my great God, that he hath granted unto us that
we might repent of these things, and also that he hath forgiven us of those our many sins and murders which we have
committed, and taken away the guilt from our hearts, through
the merits of his Son." (Alma 24:9–10.) In this regard, Bruce
C. Hafen has stated:

   I once wondered if those who refuse to repent but
who then satisfy the Law of Justice by paying for their
own sins are then worthy to enter the celestial kingdom.
The answer is *no*, because the entrance requirements for
celestial life are simply higher than merely satisfying the
Law of Justice. For that reason, paying for our sins [our

works] will not bear the same fruit as repenting of our sins [receiving the gift of grace offered through the Savior's atonement]. Justice is a law of balance and order and it must be satisfied, either through our payment or his. But if we decline the Savior's invitation to let him carry our sins and then satisfy Justice by ourselves, we will not yet have experienced that complete rehabilitation that can occur through a combination of divine assistance and genuine repentance. Working together, those forces have the power permanently to change our hearts and our lives. . . .

The doctrines of mercy and repentance are rehabilitative, not retributive in nature. The Savior asks for our repentance not merely in compensation to him for paying our debt to Justice, but also as a way of inducing us to undergo the process of development that will make our nature divine, giving us the capacity to live the celestial law. "The natural man" will remain an enemy of God forever—even after paying for his own sins—unless he also "becometh a saint through the atonement of Christ the Lord, and becometh as a child." As King Benjamin here suggests, the atonement does more than pay for our sins. It also is the agent through which we develop a saintly nature. ("Beauty for Ashes: The Atonement of Jesus Christ," pp. 10, 11.)

The prophet Moroni described those among the Nephites who had accepted the gospel and received the ordinances of salvation. Of them he said: "After they had been received unto baptism, and were wrought upon and cleansed by the power of the Holy Ghost, they were numbered among the people of the church of Christ; and their names were taken, that they might be remembered and nourished by the good word of God, to keep them in the right way, to keep them continually watchful unto prayer, relying alone upon the merits of Christ, who was the author and the finisher of their faith" (Moroni 6:4).

"Because we lack the power to compensate fully for the effects of our transgressions, we are utterly dependent on

Christ, no matter how earnest our repentance. Once that dawns on us, how exquisite it is to discover that the divine Redeemer truly will liberate repentant captives from the bondage of sin." (Hafen, "Beauty for Ashes," p. 12.) Indeed, the Saints in all ages receive with delight and overwhelming gratitude the words and works of Christ with unshaken faith in the Lord their Redeemer, "relying wholly upon the merits of him who is mighty to save" (2 Nephi 31:19).

And in nothing doth man offend God, or against none is his wrath kindled, save those who confess not his hand in all things, and obey not his commandments.

—D&C 59:21

CHAPTER 4

Acknowledging His Hand in All Things

When man focuses unduly upon himself and his own accomplishments he is unable to look to the source from whence his blessings spring; he is unable to focus on Christ the Lord. And thus "in nothing doth man offend God, or against none is his wrath kindled, save those who confess not his hand in all things, and obey not his commandments" (D&C 59:21).

Surely God's wrath is not kindled against the ungrateful because Deity in some way feels slighted, or because his feelings have been hurt, or because he needs our attention and our affections. God is an independent being and is possessed of all virtues and noble attributes in perfection. Insecurity is not characteristic of him who is Eternal. Nor is moodiness or pouting. His wrath is kindled against ungrateful man because such a one is worshiping a false god, and because allegiance to any object other than the true and living God is fruitless and unproductive: it cannot lead to life and salvation. When, however, men and women "thank the Lord [their] God in all things" (D&C 59:7), they are on a course which can lead them toward the realization of the measure of their creation and thus to happiness and fulfillment. Such persons—those who thank the Lord in all things, who acknowledge the Lord's hand in all things—are also those who acknowledge and gratefully accept and strive to keep his commandments. A vital part of accepting the grace of God is coming to see the hand of God in our lives.

Perceiving God's Involvement

Spiritual maturity means coming to see things "as they really are," and "as they really will be" (Jacob 4:13; compare D&C 93:24)—to see things as God sees them. The more a man or woman receives and cultivates the spirit of inspiration —the more nearly he or she gains "the mind of Christ" (1 Corinthians 2:16)—the more readily that person sees the workings of the Almighty in all phases of life. President George Q. Cannon thus observed:

You take two persons, one who has the Spirit of God, whose mind is enlightened by that Spirit—the spirit of revelation, the same spirit that rested upon the prophets who wrote the revelations and prophecies we have—you take a man of that kind, and then take another who has none of that spirit, and put the two together, and the one man's eyes will be open to see the hand of God in all these events; he will notice his movements and his providence in everything connected with his work and they will be testimonies to him to strengthen his faith and furnish his mind with continual reasons for giving thanks to and worshipping God; while the man, who has not the spirit of God, will see nothing Godlike in the occurrences: nothing which he will view as supernatural. . . . his eyes will be closed, his heart will be hardened, and to all the evidences of the divinity of these things he will be impenetrable. (*Journal of Discourses*, 21:267.)

Those who acknowledge the hand of God in all things, and abide in his commandments, are the only ones who will sustain the principles of truth and purity (*Journal of Discourses*, 8:115).

President Joseph F. Smith also reminds us that the Almighty has "raised up philosophers among [men], teachers of men, to set the example, and to develop the mind and understanding of the human race in all nations of the world. God did it, but the world does not give credit to God, but gives it to men, to heathen philosophers. They give credit to them. I give it to God. And I tell you God knew the truth before they did, and through revelation they got it [Alma 29:8]. Let me say to you, my fellow workers in the cause of Zion, do not forget to acknowledge the hand of God in all things." (*Young Woman's Journal*, June 1907, pp. 312–13.) President Smith's son, Joseph Fielding Smith, taught over sixty years later:

> We see a man with extraordinary gifts, or with great intelligence, and he is instrumental in developing some great principle. He and the world ascribe his great genius and wisdom to himself. He attributes his success to his own energies, labor, and mental capacity. He does not acknowledge the hand of the Lord in anything connected with his success, but ignores him altogether and takes the honor to himself. This will apply to almost all the world. In all the great modern discoveries in science, in the arts, in mechanics, and in all the material advancement of the age, the world says, "We have done it." The individual says, "I have done it," and he gives no honor or credit to the Lord. (Conference Report, October 1969, p. 110.)

Grateful souls are usually also discerning souls—they perceive that not all of the doings, events, and consequences of life stem from God or may be traced to his Almighty hand. So much of the suffering and pain and agony of mortality is tied to man's inhumanity to man, or to the otherwise faulty use of agency. The First Presidency early in this century explained:

> The agency of man is not interfered with by Divine Providence. . . . God, doubtless, could avert war, prevent crime, destroy poverty, chase away darkness, overcome error, and make all things bright, beautiful and joyful. But this would involve the destruction of a vital and fundamental attribute in man, the right of agency. It is for the benefit of His sons and daughters that they become acquainted with evil as well as good, with darkness as well as light, with error as well as truth, and with the results of the infraction of eternal laws. Therefore He has permitted the evils which have been brought about by the acts of His creatures, but will control their ultimate results for His own glory and the progress and exaltation of His sons and daughters when they have learned obedience by the things they suffer. . . . The foreknowledge of God does not imply His action in bringing about that which man does or refuses to do. The comprehension of this principle makes clear many questions that puzzle the uninformed as to the power and works of Deity. (*Deseret News,* 19 December 1914.)

Trusting in His Mighty Arm

To acknowledge the Lord's hand is to acknowledge his omnipotence as well as the powerlessness and impotence of unillumined man. "O Lord," Nephi cried out in poignant soliloquy, "I have trusted in thee, and I will trust in thee forever. I will not put my trust in the arm of flesh; for I know that cursed is he that putteth his trust in the arm of flesh. Yea, cursed is he that putteth his trust in man or maketh flesh his arm." (2 Nephi 4:34; compare Jeremiah 17:5.) In fact, the fulness of the gospel was restored to the earth in our day in order to bring about that which the prophets had foretold: "The weak things of the world shall come forth and break down the mighty and strong ones, that man should not counsel his fellow man, neither trust in the arm of flesh—but that every man [armed with righteousness and clothed upon with the mantle of the Holy Spirit] might speak in the name of God the Lord, even the Savior of the world; that faith also might increase in the earth; that mine everlasting covenant might be established" (D&C 1:19–22). Those who fail to receive the gifts of grace proffered by God, who fail to acknowledge the divine in their lives, "seek not the Lord to establish his righteousness, but every man walketh in his own way, and after the image of his own god" (D&C 1:16). The early Saints were sorely chastened by the Lord, therefore, and told that they had "many things to do and to repent of; for behold, your sins have come up unto me, and are not pardoned, because you seek to counsel in your own ways" (D&C 56:14).

The Saints of the Most High come to acknowledge the hand of God when they forsake the flatteries and fineries of the world, pay the appropriate dues of discipleship, and forfeit their own will to him who is both omniscient and all-loving. They become "prisoners of Christ" (Ephesians 3:1; Philemon 1:1)—they have waged a mighty warfare against the flesh and the powers of evil and have surrendered their all to the Lord of Hosts. "True discipleship," Elder Neal A. Maxwell has written, "is for volunteers only. Only volunteers will trust the Guide sufficiently to follow Him in the dangerous ascent which only He can lead." He continues:

> If instead of surrendering to Him we surrender to ourselves, we are surely bowing before an unjust and unwise emperor.
> There can be no conditions attached to unconditional surrender to God. Unconditional surrender means we cannot keep our obsessions, possessions, or cheering constituencies. Even our customized security blankets must go.
> Does this sound too severe and too sacrificing? If so, it is only until we realize that if we yield to Him, He will give us everything He has (D&C 84:38). Anyone, for ex-

ample, who prepares to sit down at that culminating banquet with Jesus, Abraham, Isaac, and Jacob, certainly would not bring along his own beef jerky. Nor would he send an advance press agent to tout his accomplishments to that special company and in the presence of Him who trod the winepress alone (D&C 76:107).

Our personal trinkets, if carried even that far, are to be left outside at the doorstep or in the courtyard, where such clutter and debris would indicate the shedding of selfishness.

Some of us nevertheless feel as though we own ourselves, our time, our talents, and our possessions; these are signs of our self-sufficiency. Actually, God lends us breath and sustains us from moment to moment (Mosiah 2:21). Even our talents are gifts from Him. Whatever our possessions, these are merely on loan to us as accountable stewards. Possessions are not portable anyway. The submissive realize this. (*"Not My Will, But Thine,"* pp. 89, 92–93.)

To acknowledge his hand is thus to admit that we are not our own; we are "bought with a price" (1 Corinthians 6:20). As one careful observer wisely pointed out, "The one principle of hell is: I am my own!" (George MacDonald, *George MacDonald: An Anthology*, p. 88.) True Saints, those with a hope in Christ, those who are pointed toward the highest heaven, know well that they are a peculiar—a *purchased* —people; they have been bought with the precious blood of the sinless Son of Man. Those who desire to be numbered among his flock gladly and gratefully acknowledge this.

Joseph Smith, the Prophet-Seer of this final dispensation, was and is a marvelous example of one whose will was swallowed up in the will of God. In writing to his beloved Emma, he remarked: "God is my friend. In him I shall find comfort. I have given my life into his hands. I am prepared to go at his call. I desire to be with Christ. I count not my life dear to me, only to do his will." (From Smith, *Personal Writings*, p. 239, punctuation provided.)

Finally, to acknowledge the Lord's hand in all things is to admit and attest that the Lord Omniscient has a plan and a divine design for his children and a timetable for when things are to come to pass. To acknowledge the hand of God, therefore, is to be patient and persevering, to be flexible and faithful, knowing assuredly that "all things work together for good to them that love God" and trust in his purposes (Romans 8:28; compare D&C 90:24; 100:15). How true it is that "the more we become like Christ, the closer we will come to Him and the more we will trust Him. Submission, after all, is the ultimate adoration." (Maxwell, *"Not My Will, But Thine,"* p. 127.)

My grace is sufficient for thee; for my strength is made perfect in weakness.

—2 Corinthians 12:9

CHAPTER 5

From Weakness to Strength, from Grace to Grace

The fall of our first parents brought spiritual separation and alienation from things of holiness. But the infinite and eternal atonement opens the door to reunion with God through Christ. Because of our Lord's saving act, because of his perfect life and his unfathomable suffering, death, and rise to newness of life, all men and women are in a position to be reconciled to the Father. In speaking to God of the plight but the possibilities of mankind, Enoch stated: "Thou hast made me, and given unto me a right to thy throne, and not of myself, but through thine own grace" (Moses 7:59). Paul likewise pleaded with the Saints in his day: "Let us therefore come boldly unto the throne of grace, that we may obtain mercy, and find grace to help in time of need" (Hebrews 4:16). We may approach with boldness the holy throne of him who is Lord and God over all—approach with confidence or assurance that we will not be rejected—because of the mediation and intercession of Jesus the Christ, who has pleaded our cause and made the terms and conditions of everlasting salvation available.

God Grants Repentance

The return to the path of purity and peace through repentance is not simply a grand work which man must perform on his own. Once a person begins to exercise saving faith in Christ—knows of God and his attributes and knows that the course the person is now beginning to pursue is pleasing to the heavens—repentance will follow. That is to say, once a person knows the greatness and power and purity of him who is Lord, he also begins to sense the vast difference between himself and his God. But repentance is more than embarrassment. It is more than remorse. As we shall see shortly, repentance is a change of heart, a change of mind, a new direction, a new way of thinking and viewing the world. Such a course is both God-ordained and God-assisted; we cannot do it completely on our own. Rather, repentance is granted and available as a free gift to man through the Atonement; through the grace and goodness of Jesus Christ, men and women are not only entitled to repent but also are enabled to do so.

In standing before the Sanhedrin, Peter and John bore a powerful witness of their Master. "We ought to obey God rather than men," Peter said fearlessly. "The God of our fathers raised up Jesus, whom ye slew and hanged on a tree. Him hath God exalted with his right hand to be a Prince and a Saviour, for to give repentance to Israel, and forgiveness of sins." (Acts 5:29–31; compare 11:18.) Paul likewise counseled Timothy: "Foolish and unlearned questions avoid, knowing that they do gender strifes. And the servant of the Lord must not strive; but be gentle unto all men, apt to teach, patient, in meekness instructing those that oppose themselves; if God peradventure will give them repentance to the acknowledging of the truth." (2 Timothy 2:23–25.)

Since God grants repentance, it cannot be viewed as a human work alone. Thus Amulek spoke of the meaning of the law of Moses and noted that "every whit" pointed to that great and last sacrifice of the Son of God, a sacrifice which would be both infinite and eternal. "And thus he shall bring salvation to all those who shall believe on his name; this being the intent of this last sacrifice, to bring about the bowels of mercy, which overpowereth justice, and bringeth about means unto men that they may have faith unto repentance." (Alma 34:14–15.)

C. S. Lewis has written in a thoughtful way how it is that God works in man to bring about repentance:

> Now repentance is no fun at all. It is something much harder than merely eating humble pie. It means unlearning all the self-conceit and self-will that we have been training ourselves into for thousands of years. It means killing part of yourself, undergoing a kind of death. In fact, it needs a good man to repent. And here comes the catch. Only a bad person needs to repent: only a good person can repent perfectly. The worse you are the more you need it and the less you can do it. The only person who could do it perfectly would be a perfect person—and he would not need it.
>
> Remember, this repentance, this willing submission to humiliation and a kind of death, is not something God demands of you before He will take you back and which He could let you off if He chose; it is simply a description of what going back to Him is like. If you ask God to take you back without it, you are really asking Him to let you go back without going back. It cannot happen. Very well, then, we must go through with it. But the same badness which makes us need it, makes us unable to do it. Can we do it if God helps us? Yes, but what do we mean when we talk of God helping us? We mean God putting into us a bit of Himself, so to speak. He lends us a little of His reasoning powers and that is how we think: He puts a little of His love into us and that is how we love one another. When you teach a child writing, you hold its hand while it forms the letters: that is, it forms the letters because you are forming them. We love and reason because God loves and reasons and holds our hand while we do it. Now if we

had not fallen, that would be all plain sailing. But unfortunately we now need God's help in order to do something which God, in his own nature, never does at all—to surrender, to suffer, to submit, to die . . . But supposing God became a man—suppose our human nature which can suffer and die was amalgamated with God's nature in one person—then that person could help us. He could surrender His will, and suffer and die, because He was man; and He could do it perfectly because He was God. (*Mere Christianity*, pp. 59–60. See publishing detail, p. 15.)

Indeed, the coming of the great Jehovah to earth to take a "tabernacle of clay"—what the Nephites called the "condescension of God"—and to lay down that tabernacle in his atoning sacrifice was the central event of all eternity, the consummate act of mercy and grace. As Abinadi declared, because Jesus of Nazareth was both God and man, spirit and flesh, Father and Son, he could subject himself to the flesh and at the same time accomplish the will of Elohim the Father (Mosiah 15:1–4). As Alma pointed out to the people of Gideon, the Savior's mortality and his suffering were essential to the acquisition and perfection of his compassion and his empathy. "He will take upon him death, that he may loose the bands of death which bind his people; and he will take upon him their infirmities, that his bowels may be filled with mercy, according to the flesh, that he may know according to the flesh how to succor his people according to their infirmities" (Alma 7:12). From Eden's dawn to the future millennial splendor, people on earth would look to the great Mediator of all men for direction and for deliverance from the paralyzing effects of sin. And because he would come, because he would live and suffer and die and rise again, repentance was granted and was freely available. Salvation would be free.

Overcoming Sinfulness

Conquering weakness involves more than merely detailing every sin and documenting every flaw of character. It surely consists of more than devoting a designated period of time to the mitigation of our more obvious personality hang-ups. Those who repent with all their hearts are renewed in their spirits and purified in their perspectives. They gain "the mind of Christ" (1 Corinthians 2:16) and come to view things as he does. The Greek word translated as repentance is *metanoia*, from *meta*, "after" and *noeo*, "to understand." To repent is literally to have an "afterthought," or to have a "change of mind." There is a related way to view these matters. *Meta* also means "above" or "beyond," as in the word *metaphysics*. To repent, in this sense, is to gain a perspective or view of things which is beyond the natural or carnal view; it is to see things from a different view, from a higher plane.

Overcoming our weakness consists of more than conquering individual weaknesses. Paul Tillich suggested that "in relation to God, it is not the particular sin as such that is forgiven but the act of separation from God and the resistance to reunion with him. It is sin which is forgiven in the forgiving of a particular sin." (*Systematic Theology*, 3:225.) Another Protestant theologian has suggested that "there is value in the practice sometimes followed by theologians whereby they distinguish between sin and sins. When the word is used generically in the singular it describes the condition of the person who is in bondage. A symptom of sin is that a person commits sins. In the eyes of the law or of the ethical theorist, the sins are freely chosen and a person is responsible for them. But theologically speaking, we need to look past the sins to the underlying sin, the sickness that needs to be cured, the bondage from which the sinner needs to be set free." (William Hordern, *Living by Grace*, pp. 93–94.)

Weakness to Strength through Grace

Moroni was troubled by the fear that the future Gentiles would scoff at the simple plainness of his writings. But the Lord tenderly answered his concerns: "Fools mock, but they shall mourn; and my grace is sufficient for the meek, that they shall take no advantage of your weakness; and if men come unto me I will show unto them their weakness. I give unto

men weakness that they may be humble; and my grace is sufficient for all men that humble themselves before me; for if
they humble themselves before me, and have faith in me,
then will I make weak things become strong unto them.''
(Ether 12:26–27; compare Jacob 4:7.)

Those who go to the Lord in earnest and pleading prayer
—who have no thought of holding back, no desire to set the
terms of the surrender of their will—will be granted a view of
their weakness, of their fallen nature, and thus of their sur-
passing need for a Redeemer. Yes, of course they will come to
sense individual sins and tiny imperfections, but, more important, they will acknowledge before him whose is the all-
searching eye that they are unworthy and unclean. They will
desire to rid themselves and cleanse their hearts of sinfulness
as well as of sins. These supplicants petition with a fervor
known only to the hungry of soul: "O Jesus, thou Son of God,
have mercy on me, who am in the gall of bitterness, and am
encircled about by the everlasting chains of death" (Alma
36:18). They will plead with the Father: "O have mercy, and
apply the atoning blood of Christ that we may receive forgiveness of our sins, and our hearts may be purified" (Mosiah
4:2). These are the poor in spirit—the bankrupt of soul—who
come unto him. They are filled.

In order to pull us from the lofty heights of self-assurance
and overmuch self-reliance, God frequently provides weakness in the form of trials and trauma and difficulties and
dilemmas. These plights of life force us to our knees and turn
our hearts toward the divine Deliverer, the mighty Savior.
Weakness not brought on by sin or foolishness, weakness, for
example, in the form of physical or emotional difficulty;
weakness in the form of setback or delay or postponement of
plans; weakness in the form of personal limitations—such circumstances can be turned by a loving and lifting Lord into
strengths and blessings, given that the recipient of the challenge is patient and submissive and prayerful.

Some dark clouds have a silver lining; others simply bring
thunderstorms; and the person who trusts in God will have
his share of both. Behind some difficulties we will see the
hand of the Lord, will envision the particular purpose for

which we are called to suffer; behind others we will see few lessons for life but more of the same on the horizon. But the man or woman of God will have learned the patience of hope, even from the most devastating trials, declaring of God, as Job did: "Though he slay me, yet will I trust in him" (Job 13:15). The grace of him who suffered most but deserved least to suffer; the grace of him who came to give life and was put to death by those he came to save; the grace of him who, while he never displeased the Father, was left to tread the winepress alone, even the winepress of the fierceness of the wrath of Almighty God (D&C 76:107)—even he "can lift us from deep despair and cradle us midst any care." (Maxwell, *Notwithstanding My Weakness*, p. 11.) In our moments of desperation and extremity, in our time of challenge and need, his grace is sufficient for us if we trust in him. The Lord's comforting assurance to the Apostle Paul has universal application: "My grace is sufficient for thee: for my strength is made perfect in weakness" (2 Corinthians 12:9).

From Grace to Grace

With divine assistance people are in a position to receive additional attributes and powers of the Spirit through repentance and subsequent faithfulness: they may receive what the scriptures speak of as "grace for grace." "May God grant, in his great fulness," Mormon pleaded, "that men might be brought unto repentance and good works, that they might be restored unto grace for grace, according to their works. And I would that all men might be saved." (Helaman 12:24–25.) To receive "grace for grace" is to receive of the Father as we give to others. In this, as in all other enterprises in this life, Jesus Christ is our exemplar and our pattern. Of him a modern revelation attests: "He received not of the fulness [of the glory of the Father] at the first, but received grace for grace" (D&C 93:12; compare John 1:16).

One Latter-day Saint writer has provided a description of the Savior's work as follows:

Grace may be defined as an unearned gift or endowment given as a manifestation of divine love and compassion, for which the recipient does not pay an equivalent price. But though grace is unearned, it need not be unmerited. When Jesus received the attributes and powers of His Father's glory, He received grace *for* grace; that is, He received the divine endowments of the Father's glory as He gave grace to others. Service and dedication to the welfare of others, in doing the will of the Father, therefore were keystone principles in Christ's spiritual development. Jesus had also covenanted with the Father that He would consecrate the glory which He would receive and develop in others to the Man of Holiness [Moses 4:2]. Here, too, He promised to give grace in order to receive grace. (Hyrum L. Andrus, *God, Man and the Universe,* p. 206, italics in original.)

The revelation cited above continues: "And [Christ] received not of the fulness at first, but continued from grace to grace, until he received a fulness" (D&C 93:13). To grow "from grace to grace" implies a developmental process, a progression from one level of spiritual attainment to a higher. Joseph Smith thus provided a definition of eternal life as that of knowing "the only wise and true God." He further taught: "You have got to learn how to be Gods yourselves, and to be kings and priests to God, the same as all Gods have done before you, namely, by going from one small degree to another, and from a small capacity to a great one; from grace to grace, from exaltation to exaltation, until you attain to the resurrection of the dead, and are able to dwell in everlasting burnings, and to sit in glory, as do those who sit enthroned in everlasting power." (*Teachings of the Prophet Joseph Smith,* pp. 346–47.)

The revelation with which we began this doctrinal concept then establishes the meaning of worship: "I give unto you these sayings [concerning how Christ received grace for grace and grew from grace to grace] that you may understand and know how to worship, and know what you worship, that you may come unto the Father in my name, and in due time receive of his fulness. For if you keep my commandments you shall receive of his fulness, and be glorified in me as I am in the Father; therefore, I say unto you, you shall receive grace for grace." (D&C 93:19-20.) We worship God as did our Master, by serving our fellowmen and by growing line upon line to the point at which we are prepared and fit to dwell with the Father of lights.

> Perfect worship is emulation. We honor those whom we imitate. The most perfect way of worship is to be holy as Jehovah is holy. It is to be pure as Christ is pure. It is to do the things that enable us to become like the Father. The course is one of obedience, of living by every word that proceedeth forth from the mouth of God, of keeping the commandments.
>
> How do we worship the Lord? We do it by going from grace to grace, until we receive the fulness of the Father and are glorified in light and truth as is the case with our Pattern and Prototype, the Promised Messiah. (McConkie, *The Promised Messiah*, pp. 568-69.)

Peter encouraged the disciples of Christ in his day to beware lest they be "led away with the error of the wicked" and thus "fall from your own steadfastness. But grow in grace, and in the knowledge of our Lord and Saviour Jesus Christ. To him be glory both now and forever. Amen." (2 Peter 3:17-18.)

By the law no flesh is justified; or, by the law men are cut off.

—2 Nephi 2:5

CHAPTER 6

Justification by the Grace of Christ

In a revelation given at the time of the organization of the restored Church, we find the following: "We know that all men must repent and believe on the name of Jesus Christ, and worship the Father in his name, and endure in faith on his name to the end, or they cannot be saved in the kingdom of God. And we know that justification through the grace of our Lord and Savior Jesus Christ is just and true." (D&C 20:29–30.) Justification is a legal term and is used in a scriptural context to describe one's relationship to God. To justify is to acquit, to vindicate, to pronounce righteous or innocent. Simply stated, to justify is to declare or pronounce one free from sin.

Justification as an Act of Grace

Those who come with full purpose of heart to Christ through the gospel covenant receive the assurance that their

Lord will renew them in spirit—he will justify them, will forgive their sins and thereby reconcile them with the Man of Holiness. This act of justification is a gift of grace, made available by him who has the power so to do. We are not justified, strictly speaking, by our own labors, no matter how noble and righteous they may be. In fact, Paul taught, "Knowing that a man is not justified by the works of the law, but by the faith of Jesus Christ, even we have believed in Jesus Christ, that we might be justified by the faith of Christ, and not by the works of the law: for by the works of the law shall no flesh be justified" (Galatians 2:16; compare Romans 3:20; 2 Nephi 2:5). As man's part of the gospel covenant, he exercises faith in the Lord, receives the ordinances of salvation, and then agrees to live a life befitting his new fellowship with Christ.

Paul reminded the Roman Saints that "all have sinned and come short of the glory of God . . . being justified only by his grace through the redemption that is in Christ Jesus." Paul stated further, "Therefore we conclude that a man is justified by faith alone without the deeds of the law." (JST, Romans 3:23–24, 28.) In providing commentary upon these verses, Elder Bruce R. McConkie has written:

> Paul reasons and announces: All men have sinned; none, accordingly, are eligible to receive the glory of God, or in other words, to be saved. How, then, can sinners be saved? What will free them from their burden of sin and leave them clean and spotless? Or, as he expresses it, how can they be justified, meaning how can they be accounted and adjudged to be righteous?
>
> He has already shown there was no power in the law of Moses to do this, for those who had the law . . . were still in their sins. But, he proclaims, by the grace of God redemption from sin is available through Christ. Through his blood all men, Jew and Gentile alike, can gain a remission of their sins.
>
> What price must men pay for this precious gift? Not conformity to Mosaic standards, not compliance with the ordinances and performances of a dead law, but the

price of faith, faith in the Lord Jesus Christ, faith that includes within itself enduring works of righteousness, which faith cannot so much as exist unless and until men conform their lives to gospel standards.

Does salvation come, then, by works? No, not by the works of the law of Moses, and for that matter, not even by the more perfect works of the gospel itself. Salvation comes through Christ's atonement, through the ransom he paid, the propitiation he made; without this no good works on the part of men could redeem them from temporal death, which redemption is resurrection, or redeem them from spiritual death, which redemption is eternal life. (*Doctrinal New Testament Commentary,* 2:230–31.)

Stated once again, men and women may be justified, pronounced clean and innocent, through the infinite gift of the atoning power of the Lord Jesus Christ. On their part, persons exercise faith in the Redeemer, repent of their sins, are baptized by an authorized servant of God, receive and maintain the gift of the Holy Ghost, and do all in their power to remain thereafter true and faithful to the gospel covenant. "When we were yet without strength," Paul says, "Christ died for the ungodly. For scarcely for a righteous man will one die; yet peradventure for a good man some would even dare to die. But God commendeth his love toward us, in that, while we were yet sinners, Christ died for us. Much more then, being now justified by his blood, we shall be saved from wrath through him." (Romans 5:6–9.)

Pronounced clean through the atonement.

The Process of Justification

To be justified by God is to be made clean in spite of one's inability to repay the Master; to be made innocent in spite of one's lack of moral perfection. It is to be acquitted from sin through one's faith in Christ, faith which manifests itself in the works of righteousness (see Romans 2:6–7, 13; Galatians 5:6; Titus 3:8, 14). The Lord compensates for the chasm between man's strivings and God's perfection, between where a man really is (that is, in the case of one who is struggling with all his heart to comply with gospel law but falling short of the divine standard) and where he must eventually be (absolute moral perfection). But justification is both a journey and a destination, a process as well as a condition, and the heavens respond favorably (as we shall discuss more directly in chapter 9) toward the righteous desires of the heart, as though those desires were actualized. Man's direction is as vital as his geography. "A comparison may be made," wrote Sidney B. Sperry, " . . . to a man on an escalator. We anticipate that he will reach a given floor if he stays on the escalator. So a person will eventually be justified, but may be regarded as being so now, if he retains a remission of sins (Mosiah 4:26) and continually shows his faith in God." (*Paul's Life and Letters,* p. 176.)

As a vital part of the process of justification, God has made available the means by which one may not only *obtain* a remission of sins, but also *retain* that justified state from day to day. King Benjamin thus spoke: "And now, for the sake . . . of retaining a remission of your sins from day to day, that ye may walk guiltless before God," he testified, "I would that ye should impart of your substance to the poor, every man according to that which he hath, such as feeding the hungry, clothing the naked, visiting the sick and administering to their relief, both spiritually and temporally, according to their wants" (Mosiah 4:26). In the same vein, Mormon described the Nephite Christian community as those who, in contrast to the people who were proud and high-minded, "were abasing themselves, succoring those who stood in need of their succor, such as imparting their substance to the poor and the needy, feeding the hungry, and suffering all manner of afflictions, for Christ's sake, who should come according to the spirit of prophecy; looking forward to that day, thus retaining a remission of their sins" (Alma 4:13–14).

We exercise appropriate faith in our Master by involving ourselves in the work of the Master—the work of searching out and caring for the needy; the Savior's most significant blessings come in the form of justifying us and cleansing us from sin. Though a person may not be perfect in all respects, his attitudes and deeds toward his fellowmen evidence his devotion to the Lord and his desire to be in harmony with the divine will. The brother of our Lord attested that "he which converteth the sinner from the error of his way shall save a soul from death, and shall hide a multitude of sins" (James 5:20), not only the sins of the wayward, but also his own. Joseph Smith the Prophet thus explained that "to be justified before God we must love one another: we must overcome evil; we must visit the fatherless and the widow in their affliction, and we must keep ourselves unspotted from the sins of the world: for [and now notice that such Christian service and saintly attributes evidence one's faith] such virtues flow from the great fountain of pure religion, strengthening our faith by adding every good quality that adorns the children of the blessed Jesus." (*Teachings of the Prophet Joseph Smith*, p. 76.)

Justification Through the Holy Spirit of Promise

After a person has received the ordinances of salvation; after he has made covenant with Christ to follow him and keep his commandments; and when he progresses to the point at which God's ways are his ways, where Christ's mind is his mind, where he hungers and thirsts after righteousness and lives by every word of God—when he reaches that point, that person will receive the justifying seal of the Holy Ghost, the ratifying approval of that Holy Spirit of Promise which grants one consummate peace here and promises everlasting salvation with God and angels hereafter. The Saints of our day have been charged to "learn that he who doeth the works of righteousness shall receive his reward, even peace in this world, and eternal life in the world to come" (D&C 59:23).

After having been taught of the necessity for the new birth, of being reborn through water and blood and spirit, Adam was further instructed by the Lord: "For by the water ye keep the commandment; by the Spirit ye are justified, and by the blood ye are sanctified" (Moses 6:60). Elder Bruce R. McConkie has written: "The law of justification is simply this:

'All covenants, contracts, bonds, obligations, oaths, vows, performances, connections, associations, or expectations' (D&C 132:7), in which men must abide to be saved and exalted, must be entered into and performed in righteousness so that the Holy Spirit can justify the candidate for salvation in what has been done. (1 Ne. 16:2; Jac. 2:13–14; Alma 41:15; D&C 98; 132:1, 62.) *An act that is justified by the Spirit is one that is sealed by the Holy Spirit of Promise, or in other words, ratified and approved by the Holy Ghost."* (*Mormon Doctrine*, p. 408, italics in original.) Our revelations thus speak of the candidates for celestial glory as those who "overcome by faith, and are sealed by the Holy Spirit of promise, which the Father sheds forth upon all those who are just and true." Such persons are "just men made perfect through Jesus the mediator of the new covenant, who wrought out this perfect atonement through the shedding of his own blood." (D&C 76:53, 69; compare 129:3; 138:12.)

Justification and Faith in Christ

In an excellent discussion of the law of justification, Gerald N. Lund has written:

> In the scriptural sense of the term, it is impossible for a man to be justified (brought back into a proper relationship with God) by his own works, because no one can keep the law perfectly. This was the very mistake that the Pharisees fell into with regard to the Mosaic law. We sometimes smile at their tremendously careful attempts to define the law and what was acceptable to it; but if you hold that a man is brought into the proper relationship with God by his own works alone, then theirs was a logical position to take. If the tiniest infraction of the law puts one's relationship to God in jeopardy, then one must be extremely careful about any violation. The early rabbis simply carried that idea to its extreme. . . .
>
> Paul said we are justified *through* and *by* faith (see Gal. 2:16; Rom. 3:28), which is the first principle of the

gospel. In other words, faith is the principle that activates the power of the Atonement in our lives, and we are put back into a proper relationship with God (justification) as faith activates that power. There are marvelous implications in this concept. . . .

We are like a powerhouse on a mighty river. The powerhouse has no power residing in itself; the potential power rests in the energy of the river. When that source of power flows through the generators of the power plant, power is transferred from the river to the power plant and sent out into the homes (lives) of others. So it is with faith. The power to achieve justification does not reside in man. Man requires the power of the atonement of Christ flowing into him. If no power is being generated, one does not—indeed, cannot—turn the generators by hand (justification by works); but rather, an effort is made to remove those things which have blocked the power from flowing into the generators (working righteousness as a result of faith). With this background then, one can understand why the scriptures clearly stress that faith *includes* works (see James 2:17-26); that is, obedience, commitment, and repentance—these are the works of faith that open up the channels so that the power of the atoning sacrifice of Christ can flow into us, redeem us from sin, and bring us back into the presence of God. Disobedience and wickedness damn those channels. (How literal is the word *damnation!*) The righteous works in themselves do not save us. The atoning power of God saves us. But our righteous works, activated by our faith in the Savior, are the condition for the operation of that power. Thus, each of us has something to say about whether he will be able to seek the gift and power of the Atonement in his behalf. ("Salvation: By Grace or by Works?" pp. 20-21, 22-23, italics in original.)

Paul expressed beautifully the relationship between the grace of God manifest to us through justification from sin, and how our faith in Christ—which leads to righteous works —may be activated. He spoke to Titus of the love of God shown by our Savior, "not by works of righteousness which we have done, but according to his mercy he saved us, by the washing of regeneration, and renewing of the Holy Ghost; which he shed on us abundantly through Jesus Christ our Saviour; that being justified by his grace, we should be made heirs according to the hope of eternal life. This is a faithful saying, and these things I will that thou affirm constantly, that they which have believed in God might be careful to maintain good works. These things are good and profitable unto men." (Titus 3:4-8.)

We know . . . that sanctification through the grace of our Lord and Savior Jesus Christ is just and true, to all those who love and serve God with all their mights, minds, and strength.

—D&C 20:31

CHAPTER 7

Sanctification by the Grace of Christ

We glory in the saving grace of our Lord Jesus Christ, "who hath abolished death, and hath brought life and immortality to light through the gospel" (2 Timothy 1:10). The gospel is indeed the good news, the glad tidings, "that he came into the world, even Jesus, to be crucified for the world, and to bear the sins of the world, and *to sanctify the world, and to cleanse it from all unrighteousness*" (D&C 76:41, italics added). Christ came to make saints of sinners, to open the way to holiness, to reconcile mankind to the Father, the Man of Holiness, and lead back to the eternal presence all who will be led. Jehovah, who is Jesus the Christ, seeks to make of those who receive him a kingdom of priests and priestesses, a holy nation. "Be ye holy," he has commanded, "for I am holy" (1 Peter 1:16; see also Leviticus 11:44; Exodus 19:5-6).

Sanctified Through His Blood

We know "that sanctification through the grace of our Lord and Savior Jesus Christ is just and true" (D&C 20:31). Jesus Christ is the means by which men and women are sanctified, made holy and clean, and his is the only name through which fallen creatures may be renewed and renovated and lifted spiritually to that plane which characterizes him who is the embodiment of holiness. Moroni explained that ultimately, if we deny not the power of God, we may be "sanctified in Christ by the grace of God, through the shedding of the blood of Christ, which is in the covenant of the Father unto the remission of [our] sins, that [we] become holy, without spot" (Moroni 10:33).

Jesus was and is the light and life of the world, and "the life of the flesh is in the blood . . . for it is the blood that maketh an atonement for the soul" (Leviticus 17:11). Thus it is that the Lord explained to Adam: "By the water ye keep the commandment [the commandment to be baptized]; by the Spirit [the cleansing agent, the Holy Ghost] ye are justified, and by the blood [the "precious blood of Christ, as of a lamb without blemish and without spot" (1 Peter 1:19)] ye are sanctified" (Moses 6:60). The scriptural record says of the great prophet Enoch: "Enoch looked; and from Noah, he beheld all the families of the earth; and he cried unto the Lord, saying: When shall the day of the Lord come? When shall the blood of the Righteous be shed, that all that mourn may be sanctified and have eternal life?" The Lord God responded: "It shall be in the meridian of time, in the days of wickedness and vengeance." (Moses 7:45–46.) Truly, as the resurrected Savior stated to his American continent Hebrews, "no unclean thing can enter into [God's] kingdom; therefore nothing entereth into his rest save it be those who have washed their garments in my blood, because of their faith, and the repentance of all their sins, and their faithfulness unto the end" (3 Nephi 27:19).

Sanctified by the Spirit

To be *justified* is to be pronounced clean, to be decreed innocent, to be delivered and protected from the demands of God's justice, to be free from sin. This comes as one exercises faith in Christ and enters into a covenant relationship with him who is the Mediator of the new covenant. But the actual cleansing, the literal purification, does not take place through water baptism alone. Rather, one must receive the baptism of fire and the Holy Ghost in order to begin the process of sanctification. Nephi explained: "Wherefore, do the things which I have told you I have seen that your Lord and your Redeemer should do; for, for this cause have they been shown unto me, that ye might know the gate by which ye should enter. For the gate by which ye should enter is repentance and baptism by water; and then cometh a remission of your sins by fire and by the Holy Ghost" (2 Nephi 31:17; compare 3 Nephi 12:2).

Moroni observed, in speaking of those who came into the true Church, that "after they had been received unto baptism, and were wrought upon and cleansed by the power of the Holy Ghost, they were numbered among the people of the church of Christ" (Moroni 6:4). "Sins are remitted," Elder Bruce R. McConkie has written, "not in the waters of baptism, as we say in speaking figuratively, but when we receive the Holy Ghost. It is the Holy Spirit of God that erases carnality and brings us into a state of righteousness. We become clean when we actually receive the fellowship and companionship of the Holy Ghost. It is then that sin and dross and evil are burned out of our souls as though by fire. The baptism of the Holy Ghost is the baptism of fire." (*A New Witness for the Articles of Faith*, p. 290; see also p. 239; *Teachings of the Prophet Joseph Smith*, p. 314.)

Likewise Elder Orson Pratt explained that "the baptism of the Holy Ghost cannot be dispensed with by the believer, any more than the baptism of water. To be born of the water, only justifies the sinner of past sins; but to be born, afterwards, of the Holy Ghost, sanctifies him and prepares him for spiritual blessings in this life, and for eternal life in the world to come." (From N. B. Lundwall, comp., *A Compilation Con-*

taining the Lectures on Faith . . . Also a Treatise on True Faith by Orson Pratt . . ., p. 88.)

Though the scriptures affirm repeatedly that it is by the purifying blood of the Messiah that men are sanctified and made pure, holy writ also attests that the medium through which this sanctification is accomplished is the Holy Ghost. Alma, in speaking to the Nephite people of the Church, proposed a series of questions that might serve as a type of spiritual checklist. One of those questions was: "Will ye persist in supposing that ye are better one than another; yea, will ye persist in the persecution of your brethren, who humble themselves and do walk after the holy order of God, wherewith they have been brought into this church, having been sanctified by the Holy Spirit, and they do bring forth works which are meet for repentance—yea, and will you persist in turning your backs upon the poor, and the needy, and in withholding your substance from them?" (Alma 5:54–55.) Christ taught the Nephites that "this is the commandment: Repent, all ye ends of the earth, and come unto me and be baptized in my name, that ye may be sanctified by the reception of the Holy Ghost, that ye may stand spotless before me at the last day" (3 Nephi 27:20; compare D&C 84:33).

"Strictly speaking, men are sanctified by the Spirit, and they are justified by the Spirit; but in a larger sense, they are sanctified by the blood, and they are justified by the blood, because the blood of Christ (meaning his atonement, wherein he shed his blood) is the foundation upon which all things rest. Thus, by way of accurate exposition, we are justified by the Spirit because of the blood of Christ." (McConkie, *Doctrinal New Testament Commentary*, 2:239.)

Free from the Effects of Sin

To be justified is to be free from sin, to be legally right before God. To be sanctified is to be free from the *effects* of sin, to have had sinfulness and the enticements of sin rooted out of our hearts and desires. To be sanctified in regard to vice is to shudder and shake at its appearance, to feel a revulsion for whatever allurements would detour or detain the human heart. It is to be as Jacob was: "Behold," he said, "my soul abhorreth sin, and my heart delighteth in righteousness" (2 Nephi 9:49; compare 4:31; Jacob 2:5). It is to be like the ancient people of God described by Alma: "They were called after this holy order [after the order of the high priesthood], and were sanctified, and their garments were washed white through the blood of the Lamb. Now they, after being sanctified by the Holy Ghost, having their garments made white, being pure and spotless before God, could not look upon sin save it were with abhorrence; and there were many, exceedingly great many, who were made pure and entered into the rest of the Lord their God." (Alma 13:11–12.)

Orson Pratt has provided an insightful look into the nature of being sanctified by the Spirit through the blood of Christ:

Water Baptism is only a preparatory cleansing of the believing penitent; it is only a condition of a cleansing from sin; whereas, the Baptism of fire and the Holy Ghost cleanses more thoroughly, by renewing the inner man, and by purifying the affections, desires, and thoughts which have long been habituated in the impure ways of sin.

Without the aid of the Holy Ghost, a person . . . would have but very little power to change his mind, at once, from its habituated course, and to walk in newness of life. Though his sins may have been cleansed away, yet so great is the force of habit, that he would, without being renewed by the Holy Ghost, be easily overcome, and contaminated again by sin. Hence, it is infinitely important that the affections and desires should be, in a measure, changed and renewed, so as to cause him to hate that which he before loved, and to love that which he before hated: to thus renew the mind of man is the work of the Holy Ghost. ("The Holy Spirit," pp. 56–57.)

This change of nature, change of personality, change of desires and passions, is accomplished through the purging powers of the Holy Ghost. But it is accomplishable because of the atoning blood of Jesus Christ. A modern prophet, Ezra Taft Benson, has reminded us: "The Lord works from the inside out. The world works from the outside in. The world would take people out of the slums. Christ takes the slums out of people, and then they take themselves out of the slums. The world would mold men by changing their environment. Christ changes men, who then change their environment. The world would shape human behavior, but Christ can change human nature. . . . Yes, Christ changes men, and changed men can change the world. Men changed by Christ will be captained by Christ. . . . Finally, men captained by Christ will be consumed in Christ." (Conference Report, October 1985, pp. 5–6.)

Let the Sanctified Take Heed

In a revelation given at the time of the organization of the latter-day Church, the Saints learned: "There is a possibility that man may fall from grace and depart from the living God; therefore let the church take heed and pray always, lest they fall into temptation; yea, and even let those who are sanctified take heed also" (D&C 20:32–34). Though one has gotten onto that strait and narrow path which leads to life; though one has navigated that path and partaken of the fruits of the atonement of Jesus Christ and known the consummate joys of acceptance into the fold and fellowship with the Saints; though one has risen to levels of spiritual grace wherein he has partaken of the fruits and blessings of the Spirit—despite these experiences there is a critical need for one to be "steadfast and immovable, always abounding in good works" (Mosiah 5:15), enduring faithfully to the end of one's mortal days. Even those members of the Church who have enjoyed the sanctifying and cleansing blessings of the Spirit need to guard their attitudes and their actions, to watch and pray continually, lest they "fall from grace."

In one sense, Saints of the Most High fall from grace whenever they commit sin, for in so doing they separate themselves temporarily from the Spirit of God and rob themselves of that direction and comfort available through sustained righteousness. But, as we shall see in chapter 10, no man or woman will achieve the ultimate, the ideal, of perfection in this life, though the Saints are under covenant to strive for that goal. And thus it is that the process of justification, made possible through the ransoming and mediating power of our Lord and Savior—available to us as Latter-day Saints as we involve ourselves in Christian service and deeds of faith and righteousness—allows us the privilege of turning regularly to him who is mighty to save and of thus retaining a remission of sins from day to day.

There is also a scriptural sense in which those who have made sure their calling and election to eternal life—have received the assurance and promise of exaltation—are designated as the sanctified. "There has been a day of calling," a revelation declared, "but the time has come for a day of choosing; and let those be chosen that are worthy. And it shall be manifest unto my servant, by the voice of the Spirit, those that are chosen; and they shall be sanctified." (D&C 105:35-36.) In offering an insightful commentary upon these verses, Elder McConkie has written: "Many are called to the Lord's work, but few are chosen for eternal life. So that those who are chosen may be sealed up unto eternal life, the scripture says [cites D&C 105:36]. They are chosen by the Lord, but the announcement of their calling and election is delivered by the Spirit." (*A New Witness for the Articles of Faith*, p. 270.) Should a person forsake the faith and fall prey to the spirit of bitter apostasy after having risen to this supernal level—something which would be highly unusual, inasmuch as one's disposition toward willful sin decreases with continued faithfulness—then such a person would definitely have "fallen from grace."

"It is impossible," Paul wrote, "for those who were once enlightened, and have tasted of the heavenly gift, and were made partakers of the Holy Ghost, and have tasted the good word of God, and the powers of the world to come, if they shall fall away, to renew them again unto repentance; seeing they crucify to themselves the Son of God afresh, and put him to an open shame." Paul described such a person as one who had "trodden under foot the Son of God," a person who had "counted the blood of the covenant, wherewith he was sanctified, an unholy thing, and hath done despite unto the Spirit of grace." (Hebrews 6:4-6; 10:29.) Joseph Smith explained:

> There is a superior intelligence bestowed upon such as obey the Gospel with full purpose of heart, which, if sinned against, the apostate is left naked and destitute of the Spirit of God, and he is, in truth, nigh unto cursing, and his end is to be burned. When once that light which was in them is taken from them, they become as much darkened as they were previously enlightened, and then, no marvel, if all their power should be enlisted against the truth, and they, Judas like, seek the destruction of those who were their greatest benefactors. What nearer friend on earth, or in heaven, had Judas than the Savior? And his first object was to destroy Him. (*Teachings of the Prophet Joseph Smith*, p. 67.)

In Joseph Smith's day a theological debate raged between those who believed in the predestination of souls—and thus that men and women were called and chosen, elected, to salvation from the foundation of the world and thus could not "fall from grace"—and those who believed that man had a major role in the salvation process and therefore could periodically fall from that level of divine acceptance. Only three months before his death, the Prophet made the following remarks concerning this doctrinal controversy:

> The doctrine that the Presbyterians and Methodists have quarreled so much about—once in grace, always in grace [the Presbyterians], or falling away from grace [the Methodists], I will say a word about. They are both wrong. Truth takes a road between them both, for while the Presbyterian says: "Once in grace, you cannot fall"; the Methodist says: "You can have grace today, fall from it tomorrow, next day have grace again; and so follow on, changing continually." But the doctrine of the

Scriptures and the spirit of Elijah would show them both false, and take a road between them both; for, according to the Scripture, if men have received the good word of God, and tasted of the powers of the world to come, if they shall fall away, it is impossible to renew them again, seeing they have crucified the Son of God afresh, and put Him to an open shame; so there is a possibility of falling away; you could not be renewed again, and the power of Elijah cannot seal against this sin [the unpardonable sin, the sin against the Holy Ghost], for this is a reserve made in the seals and power of the Priesthood. (*Teachings of the Prophet Joseph Smith,* pp. 338–39.)

In short, though it is true that men and women may fall from grace periodically as they climb the path to celestial life, there is a level of transcendent grace—a height toward which the Saints aspire and press with patient maturity and steadfastness—a summit which, when once scaled, necessitates that one show even greater vigilance and readiness against the onslaughts of the destroyer. Indeed, the price to be paid —no matter what the level of our spiritual attainments—is to remain faithful and true to our covenants and our commitments to the end of our days. If we leave this life firm in the faith, in good standing and in full fellowship, we will not "fall from grace" in the world of spirits or any time thereafter. Rather, we will continue in that same direction, with perhaps even greater intensity, among persons of like disposition and will go on to the highest and greatest of eternal rewards. "And if you keep my commandments and endure to the end," the Lord has reminded us in this day, "you shall have eternal life, which gift is the greatest of all the gifts of God" (D&C 14:7).

Sanctification is a condition. And sanctification is a process. It comes in time to those who yield their hearts to God (Helaman 3:35), to those whose minds are single to God and his glory (D&C 88:67–68), to those who trust in and seek after the redeeming grace of him who calls his people to the way of holiness. "Those who go to the celestial kingdom of heaven,"

Elder McConkie explained to Brigham Young University students, "have to be sanctified, meaning that they become clean and pure and spotless. They've had evil and sin and iniquity burned out of their souls as though by fire. . . . It is a process. Nobody is sanctified in an instant, suddenly. But if we keep the commandments and press forward with steadfastness after baptism, then degree by degree and step by step we sanctify our souls until that glorious day when we're qualified to go where God and angels are." ("Jesus Christ and Him Crucified," p. 399.)

After ye are reconciled unto God, . . . it is only in and through the grace of God that ye are saved.

—2 Nephi 10:24

CHAPTER 8

Grace and Works: The Essential Balance

Confusion and uncertainty continue to exist in the minds of people throughout the world concerning the Latter-day Saints' view of Jesus Christ and the work of redemption. Much of this confusion is no doubt reflected in the conclusion by some that the Latter-day Saints are not Christian. Though it is difficult to fathom how people who are at least vaguely familiar with the Book of Mormon could draw such conclusions, accusations and innuendos persist.

By Grace or by Works?

A typical description of the Latter-day Saint view of Christ and the Atonement is contained in the following paragraph written some years ago by the religion editor of a prominent national magazine:

In Mormon scriptures, the story of Adam and Eve is accepted as literal truth. . . . According to Mormon tradition, not only did Adam's fall make procreation possible, it also established the conditions for human freedom and moral choice. Unlike orthodox Christians, *Mormons believe that men are born free of sin and earn their way to godhood by the proper exercise of free will, rather than through the grace of Jesus Christ. Thus Jesus' suffering and death in the Mormon view were brotherly acts of compassion, but they do not atone for the sins of others.* For this reason, Mormons do not include the cross in their iconography nor do they place much emphasis on Easter. (Kenneth L. Woodward, "What Mormons Believe," p. 68, italics added.)

It is frustrating and terribly unfortunate that we as a church should be so misrepresented. It is sad that persons should fail to see in our lives as well as our literature that Jesus Christ is the focus of our faith and his atonement the fundamental principle of our religion (see *Teachings of the Prophet Joseph Smith*, p. 121). Such attitudes—that Mormons are not Christian or that we do not believe in salvation by the grace of Christ—may be due in large part to our tendency to react (and perhaps overreact) to what we may feel to be an overreliance by Protestant Christianity upon salvation by grace.

Before leaving on a mission, for example, I approached one of my priesthood leaders with the question, "What does it mean to be saved by grace?" Having been raised in the Southern States and in the "Bible Belt," I had heard the phrase many times from numerous friends.

My priesthood leader—a powerful preacher of the gospel and one who knew the doctrines well—responded quickly: "We don't believe in that."

I asked further: "We don't believe in salvation by grace? Why not?"

His comeback: "Because the Baptists do!"

Without question, the doctrinal restoration for which Joseph Smith was the human instrument was essential in tearing away the theological cobwebs of centuries, pulling back the veil, and revealing God anew; in restoring plain and precious truths which had been lost from the Bible; and in providing doctrinal texts and contexts, a proper setting and background for understanding all other aspects of life. We need not, however, swing to extremes unnecessarily. The Baptists also believe in baptism by immersion. The Roman Catholics believe that priesthood authority is necessary for salvation. The Jews (at least anciently) believed the temple to be the central focus of community worship. We need not deny or flee from any of these doctrinal postures merely because others accept them; truth is to be found in varying degrees and forms in many forums. Although the Lord has restored to us the fulness of the gospel, we should not be surprised to find meaningful truths elsewhere in the religious world.

Some time after the article mentioned above had appeared, one person responded negatively in writing, deeply concerned that the writer could have "spent as much time as he did among the Mormons" only to come away with a skewed perception of Latter-day Saint theology. The religion editor answered the concern as follows: "I did read several books of Mormon scripture and theology before writing the article. My intent, however, was not to review books but rather to report how representative members of the LDS Church describe and interpret their own traditions. . . . The point is to determine what doctrines of a church are genuinely infused into the lifeblood of its adherents." (Cited in Hafen, "Beauty for Ashes," p. 4.)

The problem may well arise from more than bias on the part of an uninformed or hostile press, more than bigotry on the part of ministers who feel threatened by the growing Latter-day Saint presence in the religious world. It just may be that as Church members we talk of Christ too seldom, rejoice in Christ too seldom, preach of Christ too seldom, and that as a result not only our children but also many friends and bystanders do not know to what source we look for a remission of our sins (see 2 Nephi 25:26). It may be that too many are confused as to exactly where we stand on the vital issue of salvation by grace. As this work has sought to demonstrate, the scriptures and the prophets are bold in testifying of the proper relationship—the essential balance—between the merits of Christ and the merits of man. Let us now set forth some of the more salient principles associated with this doctrine.

The Apostle Paul and Martin Luther

To begin with, let us consider the types of extremes to which people gravitate in regard to grace and works. The Apostle Paul encountered at least two groups of people who needed to rely upon the works and mercies and atoning grace of Jesus Christ and rely much less upon their own labors and achievements. Envisioning that situation, Elder Bruce R. McConkie wrote:

> On the one hand, we are preaching to Jews who, in their lost and fallen state, have rejected their Messiah and who believe they are saved by the works and performances of the Mosaic law.
>
> On the other hand, we are preaching to pagans— Romans, Greeks, those in every nation—who know nothing whatever about the Messianic word, or of the need for a Redeemer, or of the working out of the infinite and eternal atonement. They worship idols, the forces of nature, the heavenly bodies, or whatever suits their fancy. As with the Jews, they assume that this or that sacrifice or appeasing act will please the Deity of their choice and some vague and unspecified blessings will result.
>
> Can either the Jews or the pagans be left to assume that the works they do will save them? Or must they forget their little groveling acts of petty worship, gain faith in Christ, and rely on the cleansing power of his blood for salvation?
>
> They must be taught faith in the Lord Jesus Christ and to forsake their traditions and performances. Surely we must tell them they cannot be saved by the works they are doing, for man cannot save himself. Instead

they must turn to Christ and rely on his merits and mercy and grace. ("What Think Ye of Salvation by Grace?" pp. 47–48.)

We thus find Paul writing, for example, to the Ephesian Saints as follows: "By grace are ye saved through faith; and that not of yourselves: it is the gift of God: not of works, lest any man should boast" (Ephesians 2:8–9).

Some fifteen centuries later Martin Luther came face to face with a mother church caught up in a system of works-righteousness as well as in an ever-growing emphasis upon the payment of indulgences. Luther struggled both with his allegiance to the church and with his own soul—ever questioning his worth and berating himself because of the pull of the flesh. In Luther's own words:

I greatly longed to understand Paul's Epistle to the Romans and nothing stood in the way but that one expression, "the justice of God," because I took it to mean that justice whereby God is just and deals justly and punishes the unjust.

My situation was that, although an impeccable monk, I stood before God as a sinner troubled in conscience, and I had no confidence that my merit would assuage him. Therefore I did not love a just and angry God, but rather hated and murmured against him. Yet I clung to the dear Paul and had a great yearning to know what he meant.

Night and day I pondered until I saw the connection between the justice of God and the statement that "the just shall live by his faith." Then I grasped that the justice of God is that righteousness by which through grace and sheer mercy God justifies us through faith. Thereupon I felt myself to be reborn and to have gone through open doors into paradise. The whole of scripture took on a new meaning, and whereas before the "justice of God" had filled me with hate, now it became to me inexpressibly sweet in greater love. The passage of Paul became to me a gate to heaven. (From Roland Bainton, *Here I Stand*, pp. 49–50.)

Luther's rebellion against Roman Catholicism and the mandatory works stipulated by that church led him into reformation, a call for the cleansing of what he perceived to be a polluted vessel. It also led him to formulate and espouse the doctrine of salvation *by grace alone* through faith alone. Millions of Protestants worldwide have come to view salvation as that which was purchased by Christ and which requires little more than confession and acceptance of Jesus as Savior.

Cheap or Costly Grace?

We are confronted today by an army of religionists who proclaim that salvation was wrought on a cross some two thousand years ago; that there is absolutely nothing that any person can do today that will impact upon his or her personal salvation other than offer a verbal profession of the Lord Jesus, a pledge of allegiance for Christ. Crusades and revivals almost without number dot the planet, nearly all of which conclude with an invitation by the evangelist to come forward, accept and receive Jesus into the heart, and acknowledge thereafter that on that occasion salvation was realized. Unfortunately, such a view of salvation has produced in hosts of otherwise earnest persons a false sense of spiritual security, has resulted in their creation of what the German theologian Dietrich Bonhoeffer called "cheap grace."

Cheap grace means grace sold on the market like cheapjack's wares. The sacraments, the forgiveness of sin, and the consolations of religion are thrown away at cut prices. Grace is represented as the Church's inexhaustible treasury, from which she showers blessings with generous hands, without asking questions or fixing limits. Grace without price; grace without cost! The essence of grace, we suppose, is that the account has been paid in advance; and, because it has been paid, everything can be had for nothing. Since the cost was infinite, the possibilities of using and spending it are infinite. What would grace be if it were not cheap? . . .

Cheap grace means the justification of sin without the justification of the sinner. . . . Cheap grace is not the kind of forgiveness of sin which frees us from the toils of sin. Cheap grace is the grace we bestow on ourselves. (Reprinted with permission of Macmillan Publishing Company from *The Cost of Discipleship* by Dietrich Bonhoeffer, pp. 45, 46, 47. Copyright © 1959 by SCM Press, Ltd.)

More recently, another Protestant minister has grown weary of what he has come to call "easy-believism." He has written:

The more I have examined Jesus' public ministry and His dealings with inquirers, the more apprehensive I have become about the methods and content of contemporary evangelism. On a disturbing number of fronts, the message being proclaimed today is not the gospel according to Jesus.

The gospel in vogue today holds forth a false hope to sinners. It promises them they can have eternal life yet continue to live in rebellion against God. Indeed, it encourages people to claim Jesus as Savior yet defer until later the commitment to obey Him as Lord. It promises salvation from hell but not necessarily freedom from iniquity. It offers false security to people who revel in the sins of the flesh and spurn the way of holiness. By separating faith from faithfulness, it leaves the impression that intellectual assent is as valid as wholehearted obedience to the truth. Thus the good news of Christ has given way to the bad news of an insidious easy-believism that makes no moral demands on the lives of sinners. It is not the same message Jesus proclaimed.

"This new gospel," the writer continues, "has spawned a generation of professing Christians whose behavior often is indistinguishable from the rebellion of the unregenerate." Thus, he concludes,

We have no business preaching grace to people who do not understand the implications of God's law. It is meaningless to expound on grace to someone who does not know the divine demand for righteousness. Mercy cannot be understood without a corresponding understanding of one's own guilt. A gospel of grace cannot be preached to someone who has not heard that God requires obedience and punishes disobedience. (MacArthur, *The Gospel According to Jesus*, pp. 15–16, 85. See copyright detail, p. 14.)

As we shall see, the grace of God, provided through the intercession of the Savior, is free yet expensive; it is costly grace, "costly because it costs a man his life, and it is grace because it gives a man the only true life. . . . Above all, it is costly because it cost God the life of his Son . . . and what has cost God much cannot be cheap for us. Above all, it is grace because God did not reckon his Son too dear a price to pay for our life, but delivered him up for us." (Bonhoeffer, *The Cost of Discipleship*, pp. 47–48. See copyright detail, p. 67.) Far too many "assume that because Scripture contrasts faith and works, faith may be devoid of works. They set up a concept of faith that eliminates submission, yieldedness, or turning from sin, and they categorize all the practical elements of salvation as human works. They stumble over the twin truths that salvation is a gift, yet it costs everything." (MacArthur, *The Gospel According to Jesus*, p. 31. See copyright detail, p. 14.)

With the restoration of the gospel through the Prophet Joseph Smith have come vital verities relative to this matter of grace and works, sacred truths which help to establish the essential but delicate balance between what God has done and what we must do.

Paul and James on Abraham: Grace and Works

One of the major theological challenges in the Christian world for centuries has been what appeared to be the apparent contradiction between the writings of Paul and the epistle of James. As we have noted above, Paul places great stress upon the need for trusting and relying wholly upon the merits of Jesus Christ and thus of accepting the gifts of grace offered through him. James, on the other hand, devotes a substantial portion of his general letter to expounding the point that "faith without works is dead." James's stress upon the necessity for works led Martin Luther to call the epistle of James "an epistle of straw" and to propose that it be deleted from the scriptural canon on the basis that it contradicted the pure gospel taught by Paul to the Christian communities of the first century.

Indeed, without the elevated and clarifying perspective provided by the Book of Mormon, modern revelation, and latter-day prophets, we would be at a loss to understand what is involved and what was intended by these two mighty servants of the Lord. In Romans 4, Paul essentially asks the question, "What was it that made Abraham such a great man? Why was he accepted of the Lord?" The answer is very simple, Paul suggests: Abraham had faith—believed God—and it was accounted unto him for righteousness. In James 2, the brother of the Lord essentially asks, "What was it that made Abraham such a great man? Why was he accepted of the Lord?" It could not have been his faith alone, James suggests. No, he contends, Abraham's faith was manifest and evident in his willingness to sacrifice his son Isaac—in his works.

In reality, it was Abraham's faith which brought the approbation of God. And it was Abraham's works which brought forth the blessings of heaven. President Joseph Fielding Smith explained:

Paul taught these people—who thought that they could be saved by some power that was within them, or by observing the law of Moses—he pointed out to them the fact that if it were not for the mission of Jesus Christ, if it were not for this great atoning sacrifice, they could not be redeemed. And therefore it was by the grace of God that they are saved, not by any work on their part, for they were absolutely helpless. Paul was absolutely right.

And on the other hand, James taught just as the Lord taught, just as Paul had taught in other scripture, that it is our duty, of necessity, to labor, to strive in diligence, and faith, keeping the commandments of the Lord, if we would obtain that inheritance which is promised to the faithful, and which shall be given unto them through their faithfulness to the end. There is no conflict in the doctrines of these two men. (*Doctrines of Salvation,* 2:310.)

Necessary and Sufficient Conditions

As we have seen already, the grace of God is a *necessary* condition for salvation; there is no way, in time or in eternity, that man could produce the plan of salvation—create himself, fall, or redeem himself—for such is the work of the Gods. But the grace of God is a gift to mankind, a gift which must be perceived and received to be efficacious. Therefore, acting alone, the grace of Christ is not *sufficient* for salvation. The works of man—the ordinances of salvation, the deeds of service and acts of charity and mercy—are *necessary* for salvation; they evidence man's commitment and fulfill his covenant with Christ to do all in his power to live the life of a Saint and overcome the world, even as he who is our prototype did. But the works of man will never be enough to qualify one for the eternal prize; acting alone, without the grace and mercy and condescension of God, these deeds are but paltry offerings and are thus not *sufficient* for salvation. And thus it is that Moroni, at the end of the Nephite record, invited us to "come unto Christ, and be perfected in him, and deny yourselves of all ungodliness; and if ye shall deny yourselves of all ungodliness, and love God with all your might, mind and strength, *then is his grace sufficient for you,* that by his grace ye may be perfect in Christ" (Moroni 10:32, italics added).

Elder Orson Pratt provided an excellent summary of the principle we are here considering.

We are to understand from [Ephesians 2:8–10], that the grace and faith by which man is saved, are the gifts of

God, having been purchased for him not by his own works, but by the blood of Christ. Had not these gifts been purchased for man, all exertions on his part would have been entirely unavailing and fruitless. Whatever course man might have pursued, he could not have atoned for one sin; it required the sacrifice of a sinless and pure Being in order to purchase the gifts of faith, repentance, and salvation for fallen man. Grace, Faith, Repentance, and Salvation, when considered in their origin, are not of man, neither by his works; man did not devise, originate, nor adopt them; superior Beings in Celestial abodes, provided these gifts, and revealed the conditions to man by which he might become a partaker of them. Therefore all boasting on the part of man [Ephesians 2:9] is excluded. He is saved by a plan which his works did not originate—a plan of heaven, and not of earth.

Well might the Apostle declare to the Ephesians, that these gifts were not of themselves, neither of their works, when the God and Father of our spirits, from whom cometh every good and perfect gift, was the great Author of them. But are these great gifts bestowed on fallen man without his works? No: man has these gifts purchased for and offered to him; but before he can receive and enjoy them he must exercise his agency and accept of them: and herein is the condemnation of man, because when he was in a helpless fallen condition, and could not by his own works and devices atone for the least of his sins, the Only Begotten of the Father gave his own life to purchase the gifts of faith and salvation for him, and yet he will not so much as accept of them. (From N. B. Lundwall, comp., *A Compilation Containing the Lectures on Faith . . . Also a Treatise on True Faith by Orson Pratt . . .*, pp. 82–83.)

After All We Can Do

In short, "however good a person's works, he could not be saved had Jesus not died for his and everyone else's sins. And

however powerful the saving grace of Christ, it brings exaltation to no man who does not comply with the works of the
gospel." (Spencer W. Kimball, *The Teachings of Spencer W.
Kimball*, p. 71.) Or to echo the glorious words of Nephi, we
encourage all "to believe in Christ, and to be reconciled to
God; for *we know that it is by grace that we are saved, after all we
can do*" (2 Nephi 25:23, italics added; compare 10:24).

President Ezra Taft Benson offered the following insightful
commentary on Nephi's phrase, "after all we can do":

> As a Church, we are in accord with Nephi, who said,
> "it is by grace that we are saved, after all we can do" (2
> Nephi 25:23). Grace consists of God's gift to His chil-
> dren wherein He gave His Only Begotten Son that who-
> soever would believe in Him and comply with His laws
> and ordinances would have everlasting life. . . . Yes, it is
> "by grace that we are saved, after all we can do" (2
> Nephi 25:23).
>
> What is meant by "after all we can do"? "After all
> we can do" includes extending our best effort. "After all
> we can do" includes living his commandments. "After
> all we can do" includes loving our fellowmen and pray-
> ing for those who regard us as their adversary. "After all
> we can do" means clothing the naked, feeding the hun-
> gry, visiting the sick and giving "succor [to] those who
> stand in need of [our] succor" (Mosiah 4:15) — remem-
> bering that what we do unto one of the least of God's
> children, we do unto Him (see Matthew 25:34–40; D&C
> 42:38). "After all we can do" means leading chaste,
> clean, pure lives, being scrupulously honest in all our
> dealings and treating others the way we would want to
> be treated. (*The Teachings of Ezra Taft Benson*, pp.
> 353–54.)

No more heinous doctrine could exist than that which encourages lip service to God but discourages wholehearted
obedience and the works attendant to discipleship. "Salvation by grace alone and without works," Elder Bruce R. Mc-
Conkie explained, "as it is taught in large segments of

Christendom today, is akin to what Lucifer proposed in pre-existence—that he would save all mankind and one soul should not be lost. He would save them without agency, without works, without any act on their part. As with the proposal of Lucifer in the preexistence to save all mankind, so with the doctrine of salvation by grace alone, without works, as it is taught in modern Christendom—both concepts are false. There is no salvation in either of them. They both come from the same source; they are not of God." ("What Think Ye of Salvation by Grace?" p. 49.)

And surely no more diabolical belief could exist than that which encourages the kind of smug self-assurance that comes from trusting in one's own works, relying upon one's own strength, and seeking to prosper through one's own genius. It is an affront to God and a mock of the atoning power of him whom God sent, for man to place himself at the center of things, for him to revel in his own greatness and marvel at his own achievements. Pure humanism is a doctrine of the devil: it places an inordinate emphasis upon fallible man and thus deflects man's vision away from the heavens and the powers of redemption. Even among some Latter-day Saints we frequently find that an overemphasis upon man as "a god in embryo" tends to underplay the effects of the Fall and thus the constant need for divine assistance in overcoming the natural man (see Mosiah 3:19). The key to understanding this sacred principle—the relationship between the grace of God and the works of man—is balance, balance and perspective provided through the scriptures of the Restoration and the words of living oracles of this dispensation.

Glenn L. Pearson offered an analogy which might prove helpful in specifying the relationship we have been discussing.

A man is wandering in a hot and barren waste, and about to die of thirst, when he is caused to look up at the top of the hill where he sees a fountain of water in a restful setting of green grass and trees. His first impulse is to dismiss it as a mirage sent to torture his weary soul. But, being wracked with thirst and fatigue, and doomed to certain destruction anyway, he chooses to believe and pursue this last hope. As he drives his weary flesh to the top of the hill, he begins to see evidence of the reality of his hope; and, renewing his efforts, struggles on to the summit where he wets his parched lips, cools his fevered brow, and restores life to his body as he drinks deeply from the fountain. He is saved!

What saved him? Was it the climb up the hill? Or was it the water? If he had remained at the foot of the hill either because of disbelief or lack of fortitude, his only means of salvation would have remained inaccessible. On the other hand, if he had climbed to the top and found he had labored in vain, he would have been worse off, if possible. . . .

The climb up the hill represents obedience to the gospel (faith in Christ, repentance, baptism of water, baptism of the Spirit, and endurance to the end); the water is that same eternal drink which Jesus offered the woman at the well. It is the atonement of Christ which is supplied as an act of grace. (*Know Your Religion,* pp. 92–93.)

President Harold B. Lee wisely taught: "Spiritual certainty that is necessary to salvation must be preceded by a maximum of individual effort. Grace, or the free gift of the Lord's atoning power, must be preceded by personal striving." (*Stand Ye in Holy Places,* p. 213.) Or, in the words of Paul, "Ye are justified of faith and works, through grace, to the end the promise might be sure to all the seed; not to them only who are of the law, but to them also who are of the faith of Abraham; who is the father of us all" (JST, Romans 4:16).

If their works were good in this life, and the desires of
their hearts were good, . . . they should also, at the
last day, be restored unto that which is good.

—Alma 41:3

CHAPTER 9

The Desires of Our Hearts

By 1831 the headquarters of the restored Church had moved
from New York and Pennsylvania to Ohio. In late 1832 the
Lord gave instructions for the establishment of a "school of
the prophets," calling specifically for "a house of prayer, a
house of fasting, a house of faith, a house of learning, a house
of glory, a house of order, a house of God" (D&C 88:119).

The course of study and pondering and prayer and faith of
the School of the Prophets anticipated temple worship and
proved to be a pattern for how all of the Saints were to come
before the Lord in sacred places in all holiness of heart. The
God of ancient Israel gave particular direction to modern
Israel that a temple was to be erected, "in the which house,"
the Lord Jehovah explained, "I design to endow those whom
I have chosen with power from on high" (D&C 95:8). The
Saints came to know that if they would give their all in sacrifice—would provide whatever time and talents and means
were required—for the building of the temple, the heavens
would be opened and their labors would be rewarded. The

Saints were obedient and the word of God was verified. There followed, especially in early 1836, a pentecostal season, an era of unusual spiritual enlightenment and refreshment.

Alvin Smith: A Scriptural Prototype

The leadership of the Church had begun meeting in the Kirtland Temple even before it was completed. On Thursday, 21 January 1836, the First Presidency, the high councils from Ohio and Missouri, and the patriarch of the Church, Joseph Smith, Sr., were engaged in a series of meetings. In the evening the Prophet took part in what came to be known as a "blessing meeting," an occasion on which priesthood blessings were bestowed and prophetic utterances made.

After the presidency had laid their hands upon Joseph Smith's head and pronounced many blessings, the Prophet was taken into vision. "The heavens were opened upon us, and I beheld the celestial kingdom of God, and the glory thereof" (D&C 137:1). The Prophet described the "transcendent beauty" and grandeur of that holy abode, including the wondrous glory of the throne of God and the streets of that kingdom. He saw father Adam and Abraham there. He also saw his mother and father, indicating that the vision was a glimpse into a future celestial world, inasmuch as both parents were still alive; Father Smith was, of course, in the same room with the Prophet. (D&C 137:2–5.) And then Joseph saw in vision "my brother Alvin, that has long since slept; and marveled how it was that he had obtained an inheritance in that [celestial] kingdom, seeing that he had departed this life before the Lord had set his hand to gather Israel the second time, and had not been baptized for the remission of sins" (D&C 137:5–6).

Alvin Smith, the oldest of Joseph and Lucy Mack Smith's children, was born in 1798. He was a noble soul, a sensitive young man solicitous of others' needs, particularly his parents'. He became seriously ill on 15 November 1823 from what Mother Smith called a "bilious colic," probably what we would know today as appendicitis. An experimental drug, calomel, was administered by a local physician. The calomel "lodged in his stomach," according to Lucy, and Alvin began to die of gangrene. He passed away on 19 November, and a pall of gloom and sorrow spread beyond the Smith home to the entire neighborhood.

> Inasmuch as Alvin had died some seven years before the formal organization of the Church (and thus had not been baptized by proper authority), Joseph wondered how it was possible for Alvin to have attained the highest heaven. Alvin's family had been shocked and saddened at his funeral when they heard the Presbyterian minister announce that Alvin would be consigned to hell, having never officially been baptized or involved in the church. . . . What joy and excitement must have filled the souls of both Joseph, Jr. and Joseph, Sr. as they learned a comforting truth from an omniscient and omni-loving God: "Thus came the voice of the Lord unto me, saying: All who have died without a knowledge of this gospel, who would have received it if they had been permitted to tarry, shall be heirs of the celestial kingdom of God; also, all that shall die henceforth without a knowledge of it, who would have received it with all their hearts, shall be heirs of that kingdom; for I, the Lord, will judge all men according to their works, according to the desire of their hearts" (D&C 137:7-9).

God does not and will not hold anyone accountable for a gospel law of which he or she was ignorant. Every person will have opportunity—here or hereafter—to accept and apply the principles of the gospel of Jesus Christ. Only the Lord, the Holy One of Israel, is capable of "keeping the gate" and thus discerning completely the hearts and minds of mortal men; he alone knows when a person has received sufficient knowledge or impressions to constitute a valid opportunity to receive the gospel message. Joseph had reaffirmed that the Lord will judge men not only by their actions, but also

by their attitudes—the desires of their hearts. (From
Millet and Dahl, *The Capstone of Our Religion*, pp.
202-3.)

Alma explained to an errant son:

> It is requisite with the justice of God that men should
> be judged according to their works; and if their works
> were good in this life, *and the desires of their hearts were
> good,* that they should also, at the last day, be restored
> unto that which is good.
>   And if their works are evil they shall be restored unto
> them for evil. Therefore, all things shall be restored to
> their proper order, every thing to its natural frame—
> mortality raised to immortality, corruption to incorrup-
> tion—raised to endless happiness to inherit the kingdom
> of God, or to endless misery to inherit the kingdom of
> the devil, the one on one hand, the other on the other—
>   The one raised to happiness according to his desires
> for happiness, or good according to his desires of good;
> and the other to evil according to his desires of evil; for
> as he has desired to do evil all the day long even so
> shall he have his reward of evil when the night cometh.
> (Alma 41:3-5, italics added; compare 29:4.)

One of the gracious acts of an omniscient Lord is his willingness to reward our righteous desires as well as our deeds.
Alvin Smith is our scriptural prototype, the classic illustration
of a righteous soul who was prohibited, because of circumstances beyond his control, from partaking fully of gospel
blessings. Elder Dallin H. Oaks has described this glorious
principle of grace as follows:

> Just as we will be accountable for our evil desires, we
> will also be rewarded for our righteous ones. Our Father
> in Heaven will receive a truly righteous desire as a sub-
> stitute for actions that are genuinely impossible. My
> father-in-law was fond of expressing his version of this
> principle. When someone wanted to do something for

him but was prevented by circumstances, he would say: "Thank you. I will take the good will for the deed."

This is the principle that blessed Abraham for his willingness to sacrifice his son Isaac. The Lord stopped him at the last instant (see Genesis 22:11–12), but his willingness to follow the Lord's command "was accounted unto him for righteousness" (D&C 132:36).

This principle means that *when we have done all that we can, our desires will carry us the rest of the way. It also means that if our desires are right, we can be forgiven for the unintended errors or mistakes we will inevitably make as we try to carry those desires into effect.* What a comfort for our feelings of inadequacy! (*Pure in Heart*, p. 59, italics added.)

To those who had not been overly endowed with this world's goods, King Benjamin spoke of their duty to the beggar: "I say unto the poor, ye who have not and yet have sufficient, that ye remain from day to day; I mean all you who deny the beggar, because ye have not; I would that ye say in your hearts that: I give not because I have not, but if I had I would give. And now, if ye say this in your hearts ye remain guiltless." (Mosiah 4:24–25.) As opposed to our legal systems in society which could never punish or reward according to motive alone, "the laws of God can reward a righteous desire or attitude because an omniscient God can determine it. If a person does not perform a particular commandment because he is genuinely unable to do so, but truly would if he could, our Heavenly Father will know this and will reward that person accordingly." (Oaks, *Pure in Heart*, pp. 12–13.)

The implications of this divine principle are especially comforting for those who seek an interest in the kingdom of God, all who aspire to holiness, who yearn to go where God is and be as he is but who wrestle with the foibles and weaknesses of a fallen world. We are able to "come boldly unto the throne of grace" (Hebrews 4:16; see also Moses 7:59), to approach the Father in the name of the Son, knowing that the God of grace will receive of our righteous desires as a fit offering. The brother of Jared thus presented himself before the

Lord with his sixteen transparent stones to receive heavenly assistance. "O Lord," he prayed, "thou hast said that we must be encompassed about by the floods. Now behold, O Lord, and do not be angry with thy servant because of his weakness before thee; for we know that thou art holy and dwellest in the heavens, and that we are unworthy before thee; because of the fall our natures have become evil continually; nevertheless, O Lord, thou hast given us a commandment that we must call upon thee, that from thee we may receive according to our desires" (Ether 3:2).

Fruits of the Spirit

The grace of the Lord Jesus is manifest not only in his mercy to us—in his willingness to receive of and judge us according to our desires as well as our works—but also in bringing about the kinds of changes in our nature that result in additional works of righteousness. That is to say, through a power beyond ourselves we begin to perform the labors and deeds which evidence a clean heart. In the world there are "works of the flesh"—immorality, witchcraft, murder, hatred, strife, and sedition; but within the community of believers there is "fruit of the Spirit," the godly walk and conversation which bear witness of Christ's power to renew and transform humanity. "The fruit of the Spirit"—the works which flow naturally from a regenerated heart—"is love, joy, peace, long-suffering, gentleness, goodness, faith, meekness, temperance: against such there is no law. And they that are Christ's have crucified the flesh with the affections and lusts. If we live in the Spirit, let us also walk in the Spirit." (Galatians 5:19-25.)

Likewise King Benjamin spoke of the manner in which the Saint—the member of Christ's church who has begun to retain a remission of sins from day to day and to grow in the knowledge and glory of God—conducts his or her life. We note that the following are not commandments and directives from a priesthood leader as much as they are descriptions of how the Saints act, how the fruits of the Spirit flow from the lives of the faithful.

And ye will not have a mind to injure one another, but to live peaceably, and to render to every man according to that which is his due.

And ye will not suffer your children that they go hungry, or naked; neither will ye suffer that they transgress the laws of God, and fight and quarrel one with another, and serve the devil. . . .

But ye will teach them to walk in the ways of truth and soberness; ye will teach them to love one another, and to serve one another.

And also, ye yourselves will succor those that stand in need of your succor; ye will administer of your substance unto him that standeth in need; and ye will not suffer that the beggar putteth up his petition to you in vain, and turn him out to perish. (Mosiah 4:13–16.)

C. S. Lewis remarked that "if conversion to Christianity make no improvement in a man's outward actions—if he continues to be just as snobbish or spiteful or envious or ambitious as he was before—then I think we must suspect that his 'conversion' was largely imaginary. . . ."

Fine feelings, new insights, greater interest in "religion" mean nothing unless they make our actual behaviour better; just as in an illness "feeling better" is not much good if the thermometer shows that your temperature is still going up. In that sense the outer world is quite right to judge Christianity by its results. Christ told us to judge by results. A tree is known by its fruit; or, as we say, the proof of the pudding is in the eating.

If "what we are," Lewis observed, "matters even more than what we do—if, indeed, what we do matters chiefly as evidence of what we are—then it follows that the change which I most need to undergo is a change that my own direct, voluntary efforts cannot bring about. . . . I cannot, by direct moral effort, give myself new motives. . . . We realize that everything which really needs to be done in our souls can be done only by God." (*Mere Christiantiy*, pp. 165, 175–76. See publishing detail, p. 15.)

Man may look upon the outward appearance, but God looks upon the heart (1 Samuel 16:7), upon the desires, upon the inner yearnings and silent pleadings of the soul. He not only sees all we do, but he knows all we feel and all we are. There is great comfort in knowing that the Lord can both perceive and purify our feelings, can both recognize and renew the desires of our hearts. Truly God "looketh down upon all the children of men; and he knows all the thoughts and intents of the heart; for by his hand were they all created from the beginning" (Alma 18:32; compare D&C 6:16).

Yea, come unto Christ, and be perfected in him, and deny yourselves of all ungodliness.

—Moroni 10:32

CHAPTER 10

Perfection by the Grace of Christ

Jesus' call to a higher righteousness, embodied in that masterful discourse we know as the Sermon on the Mount, contained the penetrating and poignant statute: "Ye are therefore commanded to be perfect, even as your Father who is in heaven is perfect" (JST, Matthew 5:50). Many months later that same Lord, now resurrected and glorified, commanded his Saints in the western hemisphere, "Therefore I would that ye should be perfect even as I, or your Father who is in heaven is perfect" (3 Nephi 12:48). This commandment to be perfect, to conform absolutely to the laws and ordinances of the gospel, did not, however, originate with Christ in the meridian of time. As Jehovah he had spoken in those terms to Abraham, the father of the faithful: "And when Abram was ninety years old and nine, the Lord appeared to Abram, and said unto him, I am the Almighty God, walk before me, and be thou perfect" (Genesis 17:1). Similarly, Jehovah commanded ancient Israel: "Thou shalt be perfect with the Lord thy God" (Deuteronomy 18:13). The directive has been given, the standard set. Nothing short of the ideal can possibly suffice: a being of absolute perfection could ask nothing less of his people.

Perfect in Our Generation

Addressing this subject, Elder Bruce R. McConkie wrote:

> *Perfection* is of two kinds — *finite or mortal,* and *infinite or eternal. Finite perfection* may be gained by the righteous saints in this life. It consists in living a God-fearing life of devotion to the truth, of walking in complete submission to the will of the Lord, and of putting first in one's life the things of the kingdom of God. *Infinite perfection* is reserved for those who overcome all things and inherit the fulness of the Father in the mansions hereafter. It consists in gaining eternal life, the kind of life which God has in the highest heaven within the celestial world. (*Mormon Doctrine,* p. 567, italics in original.)

In one sense, to be perfect is to be complete, whole, mature, fully focused. Only Jesus of Nazareth maintained a perfect walk in this life in the sense that he navigated the strait and narrow without moral detour or transgression; he alone achieved moral perfection and completed mortality without flaw or error. But others have achieved perfection in the sense that they did all that was commanded them, in the sense that they gave themselves wholly to the accomplishment of the will of the Lord. The scriptural record attests that "Noah found grace in the eyes of the Lord; for Noah was a just man, and perfect in his generation; and he walked with God, as did also his three sons, Shem, Ham, and Japheth" (Moses 8:27; compare Genesis 6:9). The same is said of Seth, the son of Adam (see D&C 107:43). Further, "there was a man in the land of Uz, whose name was Job; and that man was perfect and upright, and one that feared God, and eschewed evil" (Job 1:1).

What do the scriptures mean when they speak of a person being "perfect in his generation"? President Brigham Young explained that "we all occupy diversified stations in the world and in the kingdom of God."

> Those who do right, and seek the glory of the Father in heaven, whether they can do little or much, if they do the very best they know how, they are perfect. . . . "Be ye as perfect as ye can," for that is all we can do tho it is written, "Be ye perfect as your Father who is in heaven is perfect." To be as perfect as we possibly can according to our knowledge is to be just as perfect as our Father in Heaven is. He cannot be any more perfect than he knows how, any more than we. When we are doing as well as we know in the sphere and station which we occupy here we are justified. . . . We are as justified as the angels who are before the throne of God. (*Deseret News Weekly,* 31 August 1854, p. 37.)

We can, therefore, attain unto finite perfection, through divine assistance—through grace—in this life; that is to say, we may become *perfect in our generation,* even as were Seth and Noah and Job and all of the faithful Saints of ages past.

Means to Perfection

A careful search of holy writ affirms that there are certain activities, certain labors, which move man toward finite perfection in this life and on toward that perfection that prevails among the Gods hereafter. Paul explained that the Church of Jesus Christ—the organization, offices, councils, and ordinances—had been established "for the perfecting of the saints, for the work of the ministry, for the edifying of the body of Christ" (Ephesians 4:12; see also JST, Hebrews 6:1–2). Paul wrote to Timothy that "all Scripture given by inspiration of God, is profitable for doctrine, for reproof, for correction, for instruction in righteousness: that the man of God

may be perfect, thoroughly furnished unto all good works''
(JST, 2 Timothy 3:16-17). Paul also taught that those who
have gone before us—who were denied access to the gospel
covenant because it was unavailable to them—cannot be
made perfect without us, without our vicarious assistance;
neither can we be made perfect without the appropriate ties
between ancestry and posterity, between roots and branches
(see Hebrews 11:40; D&C 128:15). Finally, the prophets and
Apostles have repeatedly declared that patience (James 1:4)
and suffering (Hebrews 2:10; 5:8; JST, Hebrews 11:40; 1 Peter
5:10) mold men and women toward that perfection that allows them to feel confidence in the presence of him who is the
embodiment of all that is whole and complete and perfect.

Perfection and Divine Intervention

As it is with being justified, and as it is with being sanctified, perfection is both a process and a condition. But
whether we speak of a person being ''perfect in his generation'' or of that ultimate perfection which comes in and after
the resurrection, we speak of something which is brought to
pass only through the intervention of God. Man cannot justify himself. He cannot sanctify himself. And he certainly
cannot perfect himself. The transformations from a fallen
nature to a spiritual nature, from worldliness to holiness,
from corruption to incorruption, and from imperfection to
perfection are accomplished because divine powers bring
them to pass. They are acts of grace.

The Apostle Paul wrote to the early Christians: ''Now the
God of peace, that brought again from the dead our Lord
Jesus, that great shepherd of the sheep, through the blood of
the everlasting covenant, make you perfect in every good
work to do his will, working in you that which is well pleasing
in his sight, through Jesus Christ; to whom be glory for ever
and ever'' (Hebrews 13:20-21). The chief Apostle warned the
Saints late in the first century: ''Be sober, be vigilant; because
your adversary the devil, as a roaring lion, walketh about,
seeking whom he may devour: whom resist steadfast in the

faith, knowing that the same afflictions are accomplished in your brethren that are in the world. But the God of all grace, who hath called us unto his eternal glory by Christ Jesus, after that ye have suffered a while, make you perfect, stablish, strengthen, settle you." (1 Peter 5:8–10.) More specifically, people are made "perfect in Christ Jesus" (Colossians 1:28); they are "just men made perfect through Jesus the mediator of the new covenant, who wrought out this perfect atonement through the shedding of his own blood" (D&C 76:69).

Because God works upon the human soul to bring about perfection; because Deity has clearly in mind what must be done to achieve this lofty end; because the Lord knows us infinitely better than we know ourselves—for these reasons we do well to turn our lives over to him and trust in his purposes as well as his work schedule. "We may be content," C. S. Lewis has written, "to remain what we call 'ordinary people': but he [God] is determined to carry out a quite different plan."

> . . . On the one hand we must never imagine that our own unaided efforts can be relied on to carry us through the next twenty-four hours as "decent people." If He does not support us, not one of us is safe from some gross sin. On the other hand, no possible degree of holiness or heroism which has ever been recorded of the greatest saints is beyond what He is determined to produce in every one of us in the end. *The job will not be completed in this life; but He means to get us as far as possible before death.* . . .
>
> I find I must borrow . . . [a] parable from George MacDonald. Imagine yourself as a living house. God comes in to rebuild that house. At first, perhaps, you can understand what He is doing. He is getting the drains right and stopping the leaks in the roof and so on: you knew that those jobs needed doing and so you are not surprised. But presently He starts knocking the house about in a way that hurts abominably and does not seem to make sense. What on earth is He up to? The explanation is that He is building quite a different

house from the one you thought of—throwing out a new wing here, putting on an extra floor there, running up towers, making courtyards. You thought you were going to be made into a decent little cottage: but He is building a palace. He intends to come and live in it Himself.

The command "Be ye perfect" is not idealistic gas. Nor is it a command to do the impossible. He is going to make us into creatures that can obey that command. He said (in the Bible) that we were "gods" and He is going to make good His words. If we let Him—for we can prevent Him, if we choose—*He will make the feeblest and filthiest of us into a god or goddess,* dazzling, radiant, immortal creature, pulsating all through with such energy and joy and wisdom and love as we cannot now imagine, a bright stainless mirror which reflects back to God perfectly (though, of course, on a smaller scale) His own boundless power and delight and goodness. The process will be long and in parts very painful; but that is what we are in for. Nothing less. He meant what He said. (*Mere Christianity*, pp. 173–74, italics added. See publishing detail, p. 15.)

The Process of Perfection

"The path of the just," a wise man has written, "is as the shining light, that shineth more and more unto the perfect day" (Proverbs 4:18). More fully, "That which is of God is light; and he that receiveth light, and continueth in God, receiveth more light; and that light groweth brighter and brighter until the perfect day" (D&C 50:24). That is to say, we begin the process of perfection in this life, we hold to the rod of iron through fidelity and devotion to the word of truth, and we continue through the veil of death into the world to come. There we continue in our same course—loving truth, seeking light, and cherishing virtue—until in and after the resurrection, "the perfect day," we gain that perfection which characterizes those who are exalted. Concerning the process of purification and perfection a modern revelation counseled the first elders of this dispensation as follows:

And again, verily I say unto you that it is your privilege, and a promise I give unto you that have been ordained unto this ministry, that inasmuch as you strip yourselves from jealousies and fears, and humble yourselves before me, for ye are not sufficiently humble, the veil shall be rent and you shall see me and know that I am—not with the carnal neither natural mind, but with the spiritual.

For no man has seen God at any time in the flesh, except quickened by the Spirit of God.

Neither can any natural man abide the presence of God, neither after the carnal mind.

Ye are not able to abide the presence of God now, neither the ministering of angels; wherefore, *continue in patience until ye are perfected.* (D&C 67:10–13, italics added.)

We are never justified in lowering the lofty standard held out to followers of the Christ. Nor are our actions or attitudes approved of God if we suggest that the Savior did not mean what he said when he called us to the transcendent level of perfection. Our task is not to water down the ideal, nor to dilute the directive. Rather, we must view our challenge with perspective, must see things as they really are, but also as they really can be. "Pursuing the standard of perfection," one religious leader has observed, "does not mean that we can never fail. It means that when we fail we deal with it. Those with true faith will fail—and in some cases, frequently—but a genuine believer will, as a pattern of life, confess his sin and come to the Father for forgiveness (1 John 1:9). *Perfection* is the standard; *direction* is the test." (MacArthur, *The Gospel According to Jesus,* p. 192, italics in original. See copyright detail, p. 14.)

Elder Bruce R. McConkie spoke on a number of occasions about the process of becoming perfect, of the necessity of Latter-day Saints' exercising faith and having hope in Christ, and of pursuing the gospel course in a sane, balanced, and confident manner. "We don't need to get a complex or get feeling that you have to be perfect to be saved," he said to institute students in Salt Lake City. "You don't . . . have to live

a life that's truer than true. You don't have to have an exces-
sive zeal that becomes fanatical and becomes unbalancing.
What you have to do is stay in the mainstream of the Church
and live as upright and decent people live in the Church
—keeping the commandments, paying your tithing, serving
in the organizations of the Church, loving the Lord, staying
on the strait and narrow path." ("The Probationary Test of
Mortality," p. 11.) To Brigham Young University students
Elder McConkie stated: "We have to become perfect to be
saved in the celestial kingdom. But nobody becomes perfect
in this life. Only the Lord Jesus attained that state, and he
had an advantage that none of us has. He was the Son of
God, and he came into this life with a spiritual capacity and a
talent and an inheritance that exceeded beyond all compre-
hension what any of the rest of us was born with. . . ."

No other mortal—not the greatest prophets nor the
mightiest apostles nor any of the righteous saints of any
of the ages—has ever been perfect, but we must become
perfect to gain a celestial inheritance. As it is with being
born again, and as it is with sanctifying our souls, so
becoming perfect in Christ is a process.

We begin to keep the commandments today, and we
keep more of them tomorrow, and we go from grace to
grace, up the steps of the ladder, and we thus improve
and perfect our souls. . . .

As members of the Church, if we chart a course leading to eternal life; if we begin the processes of spiritual
rebirth, and are going in the right direction; if we chart
a course of sanctifying our souls, and degree by degree
are going in that direction; and if we chart a course of
becoming perfect, and, step by step and phase by
phase, are perfecting our souls by overcoming the
world, then it is absolutely guaranteed—there is no
question whatever about it—we shall gain eternal life.
Even though we have spiritual rebirth ahead of us, perfection ahead of us, the full degree of sanctification
ahead of us, if we chart a course and follow it to the
best of our ability in this life, then when we go out of

this life we'll continue in exactly the same course. We'll no longer be subject to the passions and appetites of the flesh. We will have passed successfully the tests of this mortal probation and in due course we'll get the fulness of our Father's kingdom—and that means eternal life in his everlasting presence.

The Prophet told us that there are many things that people have to do, even after the grave, to work out their salvation. We're not going to be perfect the minute we die. But if we've charted a course, if our desires are right, if our appetites are curtailed and bridled, and if we believe in the Lord and are doing to the very best of our abilities what we ought to do, we'll go on to everlasting salvation, which is the fulness of eternal reward in our Father's kingdom. ("Jesus Christ and Him Crucified," pp. 399–401.)

The children of the promise should and must have hope. For that matter, without hope there can be no true faith in Christ. "And what is it that ye shall hope for? Behold I say unto you that ye shall have hope through the atonement of Christ and the power of his resurrection, to be raised unto life eternal, and this because of your faith in him according to the promise." (Moroni 7:40–41.) Thus it is that Moroni extended the tender and timeless invitation to the Saints of God:

Yea, come unto Christ, and be perfected in him, and deny yourselves of all ungodliness; and if ye shall deny yourselves of all ungodliness, and love God with all your might, mind, and strength, then is his grace sufficient for you, that by his grace ye may be perfect in Christ; and if by the grace of God ye are perfect in Christ, ye can in nowise deny the power of God.

And again, if ye by the grace of God are perfect in Christ, and deny not his power, then are ye sanctified in Christ by the grace of God, through the shedding of the blood of Christ, which is in the covenant of the Father unto the remission of your sins, that ye become holy, without spot. (Moroni 10:32–33.)

The destination or condition of perfection is yet some distance away, but through the aid of him who is full of grace and truth, as well as through our quiet perseverance, the journey can be both meaningful and inspiring. In the language of the Prophet Joseph Smith, "Happiness is the object and design of our existence; and will be the end thereof, if we pursue the path that leads to it; and this path is virtue, uprightness, faithfulness, holiness, and keeping all the commandments of God." (*Teachings of the Prophet Joseph Smith,* pp. 255–56.) Further, President Spencer W. Kimball has declared, "the kind of life which brings happiness, brings also growth and development and leads toward perfection. Perfection is our goal, for with perfection comes exaltation and eternal life." (*The Teachings of Spencer W. Kimball,* p. 156.)

I am the vine, ye are the branches. . . . Without me ye can do nothing.

—John 15:5

CHAPTER 11

The True Vine and the Branches

Faith in Jesus Christ is the first principle of revealed religion. He is the foundation upon which we build our testimonies and the rock upon which any divine domicile is established. Helaman pleaded with his sons, Nephi and Lehi: "And now, my sons, remember, remember that it is upon the rock of our Redeemer, who is Christ, the Son of God, that ye must build your foundation; that when the devil shall send forth his mighty winds, yea, his shafts in the whirlwind, yea, when all his hail and his mighty storm shall beat upon you, it shall have no power over you to drag you down to the gulf of misery and endless wo, because of the rock upon which ye are built, which is a sure foundation, a foundation whereon if men build they cannot fall'' (Helaman 5:12).

Power in the Person

To Christ we turn in the hour of need; he is the balm of Gilead. Upon him and his word we may rely with unshaken confidence; he is true and faithful. From him we can receive the realization of our fondest dreams; his name is Eternal, and the life we may enjoy with him is called Eternal Life.

> To have faith in the name of Christ is to have an assurance, born of the Spirit, of our Lord's divine sonship, to know by revelation that no earthly man or woman—no matter how gifted and no matter how noble—could have done what He did. His work was and is the work of a God, and the product of his labors—salvation itself—is available only because of the merciful intercession of one with power over life and death.
>
> To have faith in the name of Christ is to acknowledge his hand in all things, to confess that there are labors beyond the power of man to perform. Man cannot forgive his own sins any more than he can create himself. Man cannot cleanse and renew and regenerate the human soul any more than he can resurrect himself. These are the infinite actions of a god, and they require the intervention of godly powers in man's behalf. To have faith in the name of Christ is to recognize and receive the saving grace of Christ.
>
> The power unto life and salvation is in Jesus Christ, the person. The power is not in programs, even inspired programs. Programs cannot save. They have not the power to forgive sins or sanctify or soothe troubled souls. It is the gospel of Jesus Christ which is "the power of God unto salvation" (Romans 1:16), a power which derives from him who is omnipotent. The Saints of all ages come to know by revelation the source of their salvation. . . . Christianity without the living Christ is at best deficient. Righteousness without the Righteous One cannot redeem. Theology without the gospel lacks the power of salvation. (Millet and McConkie, *In His Holy Name,* pp. 89–90.)

The Book of Mormon, which is another testament of Jesus Christ, provides a powerful pattern for members of the Church who seek deliverance from human suffering and spiritual sickness; it contains numerous illustrations of persons from the past who knew well where to turn in times of need. For example, after the people of King Benjamin had heard their prophet-leader's moving witness of the coming of the Lord God Omnipotent, they fell to the earth, "for the fear of the Lord had come upon them. And they had viewed themselves in their own carnal state, even less than the dust of the earth. And they all cried aloud with one voice, saying: O have mercy, and apply the atoning blood of Christ that we may receive forgiveness of our sins, and our hearts may be purified; for we believe in Jesus Christ, the Son of God, who created heaven and earth, and all things; who shall come down among the children of men."

We note with interest where their thoughts and their hearts were focused; we note that the center of their repentance was Jesus Christ, the person. And now we note from the account the results of their soul cries: "And it came to pass that after they had spoken these words the Spirit of the Lord came upon them, and they were filled with joy, having received a remission of their sins, and having peace of conscience, because of the exceeding faith which they had in Jesus Christ who should come." (Mosiah 4:1–3.) As the scriptures and the Apostles and prophets have always testified, the Lord's Church is an inspired and necessary vehicle; the system and organization and format for involvement in the work of the Church are divinely designed means to an end. But the Savior is the End, that toward which all things point and from which all things receive efficacy, virtue, and force here and hereafter.

Let us ponder upon the significance of another scriptural illustration. The prayers of a righteous father and a concerned community of believers in behalf of a wayward son called forth the intervention of heaven; Alma the Younger and the sons of Mosiah were struck down by an angel as they went about seeking to wreak havoc in the Nephite Church of Christ. Concerning the awful agonies of Alma's period of suffering and repentance and self-confrontation, he later explained in vivid detail: "I was racked with eternal torment, for my soul was harrowed up to the greatest degree and racked

with all my sins. Yea, I did remember all my sins and iniquities, for which I was tormented with the pains of hell; yea, I
saw that I had rebelled against my God, and that I had not
kept his holy commandments. . . . The very thought of coming into the presence of my God did rack my soul with inex-
pressible horror.''

Alma described the dramatic manner in which his soul
was turned from poignant pain to perfect peace: "And it
came to pass that as I was thus racked with torment, while I
was harrowed up by the memory of my many sins, behold, I
remembered also to have heard my father prophesy unto the
people concerning the coming of one Jesus Christ, a Son of
God, to atone for the sins of the world. Now, as my mind
caught hold upon this thought, I cried within my heart: O
Jesus, thou Son of God, have mercy on me, who am in the
gall of bitterness, and am encircled about by the everlasting
chains of death.''

Again we attend with interest to the results of such pleadings—a sincere turn to Jesus Christ for deliverance—as contained in Alma's words: "And now, behold, when I thought
this, I could remember my pains no more; yea, I was harrowed up by the memory of my sins no more. And oh, what
joy, and what marvelous light I did behold; yea, my soul was
filled with joy as exceeding as was my pain!" (Alma 36:12–
20.)

In another instance the prophet Abinadi delivered a scath-
ing denunciation of Noah and his priests, particularly of the
manner in which they feigned allegiance to the law of Moses
but failed to live in harmony with its moral precepts. Further,
he corrected their false impression that salvation could come
by the law alone. "I say unto you," he declared, "that it is expedient that ye should keep the law of Moses as yet; but I say
unto you, that the time shall come when it shall no more be
expedient to keep the law of Moses. And moreover, I say unto
you, that salvation doth not come by the law alone; and were
it not for the atonement, which God himself shall make for
the sins and iniquities of his people, that they must unavoidably perish, notwithstanding the law of Moses." (Mosiah
13:27–28.)

Elder Bruce R. McConkie suggested a latter-day application of Abinadi's words:

Suppose we have the scriptures, the gospel, the priesthood, the Church, the ordinances, the organization, even the keys of the kingdom—everything that now is down to the last jot and tittle—and yet there is no atonement of Christ. What then? Can we be saved?

Will all our good works save us? Will we be rewarded for all our righteousness?

Most assuredly we will not. We are not saved by works alone, no matter how good; we are saved because God sent his Son to shed his blood in Gethsemane and on Calvary that all through him might ransomed be. We are saved by the blood of Christ.

To paraphrase Abinadi: "Salvation doth not come by the church alone: and were it not for the atonement, given by the grace of God as a free gift, all men must unavoidably perish, and this notwithstanding the Church and all that appertains to it." ("What Think Ye of Salvation by Grace?" p. 48.)

The True Vine

One of the most meaningful allegories in scripture is recorded by John. Jesus said to the Twelve: "I am the true vine, and my Father is the husbandman. Every branch in me that beareth not fruit he taketh away; and every branch that beareth fruit, he purgeth it, that it may bring forth more fruit. Now ye are clean through the word which I have spoken unto you. Abide in me, and I in you. As the branch cannot bear fruit of itself, except it abide in the vine; no more can ye, except ye abide in me. I am the vine, ye are the branches: He that abideth in me, and I in him, the same bringeth forth much fruit: for without me ye can do nothing." (John 15:1–5.)

In offering helpful commentary upon these verses, one New Testament scholar has written:

The part of the Father here is decisive. He watches
over the vine and takes action like that of a vine-dresser
to secure fruitfulness. Every fruitless branch he takes
away. . . . Left to itself a vine will produce a good deal
of unproductive growth. For maximum fruitfulness ex-
tensive pruning is essential. This is a suggestive figure
for the Christian life. The fruit of Christian service is
never the result of allowing the natural energies and in-
clinations to run riot. . . . The man who so abides in
Christ and has Christ abide in him keeps on bearing
fruit in quantity. And the verse [verse 5] concludes with
an emphatic declaration of human helplessness apart
from Christ. In isolation from Him no spiritual achieve-
ment is possible. (Leon Morris, *The Gospel According to
John*, pp. 669, 671.)

In short, "as long as the spiritual union between Christ and
the believer, which (ideally and normally, at any rate) begins
with Baptism, is maintained by faith, love, and prayer, the
believer's soul is nourished by constant supplies of grace, just
as truly as the branches of a vine are nourished by the sap
that flows into them from the stem. Nourished by the life of
Christ, the believer's soul is cleansed, sanctified, and made
fruitful in all good works." (Dummelow, *The One Volume
Bible Commentary*, p. 800.) Those branches, on the other
hand, which fail to acknowledge the source of their existence,
which sever themselves from the mother vine or tree, which
refuse pruning and refinement, never gain the strength or
power to develop the fruit that remains (see John 15:16).

The Book of Mormon prophets spoke often of branches of
Israel being "grafted" into the mother tree. This figurative expression finds meaning only in Christ, who is the Holy One
of Israel, the God of Abraham, Isaac, and Israel. Indeed, the
restoration of Israel is first and foremost a restoration to Jesus
the Christ (Mormon 9:36). "After the house of Israel should
be scattered," Nephi wrote, "they should be gathered together again; or, in fine, after the Gentiles had received the
fulness of the Gospel, the natural branches of the olive-tree,
or the remnants of the house of Israel, should be grafted in, or

come to the knowledge of the true Messiah, their Lord and their Redeemer'' (1 Nephi 10:14). Nephi later explained to his questioning brothers:

> And now, the thing which our father meaneth concerning the grafting in of the natural branches through the fulness of the Gentiles, is, that in the latter days, when our seed shall have dwindled in unbelief, yea, for the space of many years, and many generations after the Messiah shall be manifested in body unto the children of men, then shall the fulness of the gospel of the Messiah come unto the Gentiles, and from the Gentiles unto the remnant of our seed.
>
> And at that day shall the remnant of our seed know that they are of the house of Israel, and that they are the covenant people of the Lord; and then shall they know and come to the knowledge of their forefathers, and also to the knowledge of the gospel of their Redeemer, . . . and the very points of his doctrine, *that they may know how to come unto him and be saved.*
>
> And then at that day will they not rejoice and give praise unto their everlasting God, their rock and their salvation? Yea, at that day *will they not receive the strength and nourishment from the true vine?* Yea, will they not come unto the true fold of God? (1 Nephi 15:13–15, italics added; compare Alma 16:13–17.)

Limits of Self-Reliance

Some virtues can be overdone, thereby becoming vices. Self-reliance is just such a one. We have been encouraged by the prophets for generations to become self-reliant, to avoid shifting the burden of our care or that of our loved ones to others, at least unless or until we have exhausted every possible personal or family resource. This is true in temporal, emotional, and even spiritual matters. And yet, when it comes to spiritual self-reliance, a person must use caution; he must see to it that he does not become so independent that he excludes the Lord or denies himself the power of Christ that otherwise would be his.

We must do all that we can do. We must extend ourselves to the limit, must stretch and bend the soul to its extremities. In the final analysis, however—at least when dealing with matters pertaining to spiritual growth and progression—it is not possible to "pull ourselves up by our own bootstraps," nor is it healthy to presume we can. "By His grace," President Ezra Taft Benson explained, "and by our faith in [Christ's] atonement and our repentance of our sins, we receive the strength to do the necessary works that we otherwise could not do by our own power. By His grace, we receive an endowment of blessing and spiritual strength that may eventually lead us to eternal life if we endure to the end. By His grace, we become more like His divine personality." (*Come Unto Christ*, pp. 7–8.)

With a deemphasis upon God, often there follows an overemphasis on man—his own abilities, his own strengths, his own potential. Such a humanistic view of man is accurately reflected in the now-famous poem by William Ernest Henley, "Invictus":

> Out of the night that covers me,
>   Black as the Pit from pole to pole,
> I thank whatever Gods may be
>   For my unconquerable soul.
>
> In the fell clutch of circumstance
>   I have not winced nor cried aloud.
> Under the bludgeonings of chance
>   My head is bloody, but unbowed.
>
> Beyond this place of wrath and tears
>   Looms but the Horror of the shade,
> And yet the menace of the years
>   Finds, and shall find me unafraid.
>
> It matters not how strait the gate,
>   How charged with punishments the scroll,
> I am the master of my fate;
>   I am the captain of my soul.

Elder Orson F. Whitney, a great Apostle-poet, responded to Henley as follows:

Art thou in truth? Then what of him
    Who bought thee with his blood?
Who plunged into devouring seas
    And snatched thee from the flood?

Who bore for all our fallen race
    What none but him could bear,
The God who died that man might live,
    And endless glory share?

Of what avail thy vaunted strength,
    Apart from his vast might?
Pray that his Light may pierce the gloom,
    That thou mayest see aright.

Men are as bubbles on the wave,
    As leaves upon the tree.
Thou, captain of thy soul, forsooth!
    Who gave that place to thee?

Free will is thine—free agency,
    To wield for right or wrong;
But thou must answer unto him
    To whom all souls belong.

Bend to the dust that head "unbowed,"
    Small part of Life's great whole!
And see in him, and him alone,
    The Captain of thy soul.

(*Improvement Era*, April 1926, p. 611.)

Jesus Christ is the light and the life of the world (see Mosiah 16:9; Alma 38:9; 3 Nephi 11:10–11). In him and in him alone is to be found the abundant life (John 10:10). Christ seeks to reconcile finite men with their infinite Heavenly Father. He is Mediator, Intercessor, and Redeemer. In him is the power which may be extended to fallen men and women to become the sons and daughters of God, the means whereby we may resume, through appropriate reconciliation, our status in the royal family of God (John 1:11–12; D&C 34:1–4).

We believe in Christ, not because we can see him, but because through him we are able to see all other things with such crystal clarity. As we come to view Christ as he is, we also come to view ourselves in proper perspective. In fact, the more a person devotes himself to the Lord and keeps an eye single to His glory, the more he sees that Christ is able to make of him so much more than he could make of himself with his own limited and faltering resources. "The more we get what we now call 'ourselves' out of the way," C. S. Lewis reminds us, "and let Him take us over, the more truly ourselves we become. . . ."

> I am not, in my natural state, nearly so much of a person as I like to believe: most of what I call 'me' can be very easily explained. It is when I turn to Christ, when I give myself up to His Personality, that I first begin to have a real personality of my own. . . . Nothing that you have not given away will ever be really yours. Nothing in you that has not died will ever be raised from the dead. Look for yourself, and you will find in the long run only hatred, loneliness, despair, rage, ruin, and decay. But look for Christ and you will find Him, and with Him everything else thrown in. (*Mere Christianity*, pp. 189–90. See publishing detail, p. 15.)

If our gaze is upon the Savior, we need look nowhere else. If our trust is in him and his word, we need pay little heed to the discordant voices all about us. The invitation and challenge is ever before us: "Look unto me in every thought; doubt not, fear not" (D&C 6:36).

Praise ye the Lord. Praise, O ye servants of the Lord, praise the name of the Lord.

—Psalm 113:1

CHAPTER 12

Singing the Song of Redeeming Love

Coming to know, as Moses did, "that man is nothing" (Moses 1:10) without the Lord—that we are, as Elder Orson F. Whitney observed, "as bubbles on the wave"—should create within each of us feelings not of futility but of reverent humility. We come in time to glory at the wonder and goodness and grace of our God. Indeed, how merciful he is to us!

His Yoke is Easy

The Savior's gentle invitation to the burden-weary is touching and timeless: "Come unto me, all ye that labour and are heavy laden, and I will give you rest. Take my yoke upon you, and learn of me; for I am meek and lowly in heart: and ye shall find rest unto your souls. For my yoke is easy, and my burden is light." (Matthew 11:28–30.) One writer on the New

Testament has provided the following insightful commentary upon the Lord's words:

> Jesus' hearers understood that the yoke was a symbol of submission. In the land of Israel yokes were made of wood, carefully fashioned by the carpenter's hand to fit the neck of the animal that was to wear it. Undoubtedly Jesus had made many yokes as a boy in Joseph's carpenter shop in Nazareth. This was a perfect illustration for salvation. The yoke worn by the animal to pull a load was used by the master to direct the animal.
>
> The yoke also signified discipleship. When our Lord added the phrase "and learn from Me," the imagery would have been familiar to Jewish listeners. In ancient writings, a pupil who submitted himself to a teacher was said to take the teacher's yoke. One writer records this proverb: "Put your neck under the yoke and let your soul receive instruction." Rabbis spoke of the yoke of instruction, the yoke of the Torah, and the yoke of the law. . . .
>
> The yoke of the law, the yoke of human effort, the yoke of works, and the yoke of sin are all heavy, chafing, galling yokes. They represent large, unbearable burdens carried in the flesh. They lead to despair, frustration, and anxiety. Jesus offers a yoke we can carry, and He also gives the strength to carry it (cf. Philippians 4:13). Therein is true rest.
>
> The yoke He offers is easy, and the burden He gives is light, because He is meek and lowly. Unlike the Pharisees and scribes, He does not desire to oppress us. He does not want to pile burdens on us we cannot bear, nor is He trying to show how hard righteousness can be. He is gentle. He is tender. And He gives a light burden to carry. Obedience under His yoke is a joy. (MacArthur, *The Gospel According to Jesus*, pp. 112–13. See copyright detail, p. 14.)

It is true, writes Elder Neal A. Maxwell, that "to live so as to please Him is a rigorous undertaking. But His burden is light compared to the burdens of sin, insincerity, vanity, and hypocrisy. His burden is bearable because, once we shoulder it and it alone, we can, mercifully, leave so much else behind." (*We Will Prove Them Herewith*, p. 105.)

The Master does not always remove every burden of life, every care, from our shoulders. Rather, he frequently provides for us that assistance, that strength—shall we call it grace? yes, for so it is—which allows us to bear up under what might otherwise be unbearable circumstances. For example, after Alma and his converts had fled the pestilential presence of Noah and his priests, they settled in a place which they named Helam. A Lamanite army soon overtook them, however, and Amulon, a vicious man—a former priest of Noah who knew and despised the righteous Alma—was placed at the head of the colony in Helam. "And now it came to pass that Amulon began to exercise authority over Alma and his brethren, and began to persecute him, and cause that his children should persecute their children. . . . He exercised authority over them, and put tasks upon them, and put taskmasters over them. And it came to pass that so great were their afflictions that they began to cry mightily to God." Amulon thereupon forbade the Nephites to pray and promised death to those who were caught in that act. "How bitter is the irony that so many dissipate their energies in fighting a God whose existence they refuse to admit! Had Amulon not feared the God of Alma and his people, he would not have feared their prayers. The death ban on prayer is assuredly an admission on his part of the efficacy of prayer and the reality of Israel's God." (McConkie and Millet, *Doctrinal Commentary on the Book of Mormon*, 2:287.)

Alma and his people now began to cry to the Lord in their hearts. The God of mercy and grace heard their pleas for deliverance. "Lift up your heads," he said to them, "and be of good comfort, for I know of the covenant which ye have made unto me; and I will covenant with my people and deliver them out of bondage. And I will also ease the burdens which are put upon your shoulders, that even you cannot feel them upon your backs, even while you are in bondage."

Mormon's account of this wondrous occasion follows: "And now it came to pass that the burdens which were laid upon Alma and his brethren were made light; yea, the Lord

did strengthen them that they could bear up their burdens
with ease, and they did submit cheerfully and with patience
to all the will of the Lord." (Mosiah 24:8–15.) Soon thereafter
the Lord led Alma and his followers miraculously out of dan-
ger to the land of Zarahemla, where they joined the Saints
under Mosiah.

The Song of Redeeming Love

In refocusing the minds of the Saints of his day upon their
covenantal obligations and upon the spiritual experiences
upon which those covenants were first made, Alma asked:
"And now behold, I say unto you, my brethren, if ye have experienced a change of heart, and if ye have felt to sing the
song of redeeming love, I would ask, can ye feel so now?"
(Alma 5:26.)

Alma knew well the need for continuing spiritual refreshment, for constant and current renewal of faith, and for a
growing and deepening commitment to and acknowledgment
of the Almighty God. A testimony is a fragile possession,
something which must be nurtured and fed and exercised.
We seek to establish reservoirs of faith in our lives, ever-
present sources of strength and encouragement in times of
difficulty; at the same time, we cannot forever live in the past,
cannot survive forevermore on memories, even on marvelous
and meaningful memories. Alma's question, "If ye have felt
to sing the song of redeeming love, . . . can ye feel so now?"
gets at the heart of gospel living, at the foundation of
Christlike service. One who is motivated by his love of the
Lord, his sense of overwhelming gratitude for the Father and
the Son, is prone to stay on course and seek that closeness
with the Holy Spirit which will help him to retain a remission
of sins from day to day (see Mosiah 4:11–12).

To sing the song of redeeming love is to joy in the match-
less majesty of God's goodness, to know the wonder of
God's love. It is to sense and know, by the power of the Holy
Ghost, that the Lord is intimately involved with his children

and that he cares, really cares, about their well-being; it is to relish and cherish that fruit which is the most joyous to the soul (see 1 Nephi 11:22–23). Jacob surely sang the song of redeeming love when he exulted in the wisdom of God, the greatness and justice of God, the mercy of God, the goodness of God, and the holiness of God (2 Nephi 9).

To sing the song of redeeming love is to experience that transcendent spiritual gift which the scriptures call charity, the pure love of Christ (see Moroni 7:47). It is to feel a driving sense of urgency to love and serve others purely, even as Christ does. But it is also to love Christ purely, to partake of a quality and depth of soul-love for him which knows no earthly or temporal counterparts. It is to love and honor and worship and praise the Lord as God with feelings and emotions which are unspeakable. Elder Melvin J. Ballard attempted to describe such an experience in the following words:

> I found myself one evening in the dreams of the night in that sacred building, the temple. After a season of prayer and rejoicing I was informed that I should have the privilege of entering into one of those rooms to meet a glorious Personage, and, as I entered the door, I saw, seated on a raised platform, the most glorious Being my eyes have ever beheld or that I ever conceived existed in all the eternal worlds. As I approached to be introduced, he arose and stepped towards me with extended arms, and he smiled as he softly spoke my name. If I shall live to be a million years old, I shall never forget that smile. He took me into his arms and kissed me, pressed me to his bosom, and blessed me, until the marrow of my bones seemed to melt! When he had finished, I fell at his feet, and, as I bathed them with my tears and kisses, I saw the prints of the nails in the feet of the Redeemer of the world. The feeling that I had in the presence of Him who hath all things in His hands, to have His love, His affection, and His blessing was such that if I ever can receive that of which I had but a foretaste, I would

give all that I am, all that I ever hope to be to feel what
I then felt. (*Melvin J. Ballard: Crusader for Righteousness*,
pp. 138–39.)

Similarly, Elder George F. Richards sought to explain the in-
effable sense of love and gratitude which one can feel for his
Lord and Savior:

> More than forty years ago I had a dream which I am
> sure was from the Lord. In this dream I was in the pres-
> ence of my Savior as he stood in mid-air. He spoke no
> word to me, but my love for him was such that I have
> not words to explain. I know that no mortal man can
> love the Lord as I experienced that love for the Savior
> unless God reveals it to him. I would have remained in
> his presence, but there was a power drawing me away
> from him.
>
> As a result of that dream, I had this feeling that no
> matter what might be required of my hands, what the
> gospel might entail unto me, I would do what I should
> be asked to do even to the laying down of my life.
>
> And so when we read in the scriptures what the
> Savior said to his disciples, "In my Father's house are
> many mansions: . . . I go to prepare a place for you . . .
> that where I am, there ye may be also" (John 14:2–3), I
> think that is where I want to be.
>
> If only I can be with my Savior and have that same
> sense of love that I had in that dream, it will be the goal
> of my existence, the desire of my life. (Cited by Spencer
> W. Kimball in Conference Report, April 1974, pp. 173–
> 74.)

It is not only those who have seen the Lord—have enjoyed
a personal appearance, a dream, or a vision—who feel the desire to sing the song of redeeming love, but all those who have
had the burdens of sin, the weight of guilt, and the agonies of
bitterness, hostility, or pain removed by the Great Physician.
They all shout praises to the Holy One of Israel. They all bow
the knee in humble reverence and gratitude toward him who
shall yet rule and reign as King of kings and Lord of lords.

"Peace I leave with you," he said, "my peace I give unto you: not as the world giveth, give I unto you. Let not your heart be troubled, neither let it be afraid" (John 14:27). Only through Christ the Lord may mankind know "the peace of God, which passeth all understanding" (Philippians 4:7).

Hope in Christ

We must have hope. We must have rejoicing. If any people in all the wide world have reason to be positive, to rejoice and exult in blessings unmeasured and graces abounding, it is the Latter-day Saints. If any religious body in all of creation ever had reason to look forward to the future, to prepare with joyful anticipation for that which is yet to be, it is the members of the restored Church. I am convinced that much of the discouragement that exists in the hearts and minds of some Latter-day Saints may be traced to their inability to rely on the Lord and trust in his mercies. As stated again and again in this work, we need to do all we can to prove ourselves worthy of the Lord's goodness, to seek to live the life of a true Saint. But we must also come to know that when we have done all we can—when we have stretched to the limit, have placed our offerings upon the altar of faith, no matter how meager they may seem to us at the time—we then have done what was asked of us and we will come to know that the Lord is pleased with us. Thus we need to "distinguish more clearly between divine discontent and the devil's dissonance, between dissatisfaction with self and disdain for self. . . . We can contemplate how far we have already come in the climb along the pathway to perfection; it is usually much further than we acknowledge, and such reflections restore resolve. . . . We can allow for the reality that God is still more concerned with growth than with geography. . . . This is a gospel of grand expectations, but God's grace is sufficient for each of us if we remember that there are no instant Christians." (Neal A. Maxwell, *Notwithstanding My Weakness*, pp. 9, 11.)

We feel to sing praises to the King Emmanuel with a modern Apostle who penned the following fitting and appropriate psalm:

Praise ye the Lord:
Praise him for his goodness;
Praise him for his grace;
Exalt his name and seek his face—
O praise ye the Lord.

Blessed is the Lord:
Bless him for his mercy;
Bless him for his love;
Exalt his name and seek his face—
O blessed is the Lord.

Praise ye the Lord:
Praise him who all things did create;
Praise him who all things did redeem;
Exalt his name and seek his face—
O praise ye the Lord.

Seek ye the Lord:
Seek him who rules on high;
Seek him whose will we know;
Exalt his name and seek his face—
O seek ye the Lord.

(Bruce R. McConkie, Conference Report,
October 1973, p. 57.)

A Note of Testimony

I have desired to share my feelings and my reflections upon what I believe to be the burden of all scripture in regard to the matter of being saved by the grace of Christ. Though I cannot speak for the Church, I do believe what I have written to be true and in harmony with the message of the standard works and the words of modern Apostles and prophets.

I love the Lord Jesus Christ. I know, by the power of the Holy Ghost, that he lives. I know, further, that the plan of salvation represents a gracious offering on the part of the Father, and that, as the angel taught King Benjamin, "salvation was, and is, and is to come, in and through the atoning blood of Christ, the Lord Omnipotent" (Mosiah 3:18). When I consider what love and infinite mercy is manifest by our Savior in offering himself as a sacrifice for sin, my soul wells up with deep appreciation for him who is Eternal, and my desire to express gratitude to him who bought us with his blood knows no bounds.

I know that Joseph Smith was called in this final dispensation of grace to reveal anew the Gods of heaven and to organize the Lord's Church, the church which administers his gospel. It is my testimony that The Church of Jesus Christ of Latter-day Saints is, in the language of the revelation, "the only true and living church upon the face of the whole earth" (D&C 1:30); that it is in the line of its duty and is led by prophets and Apostles called and anointed through the spirit of prophecy and revelation; and that this restored Church is the sole repository of those priesthood powers and saving truths which will allow men and women to come unto Christ and be saved in the highest heaven of the celestial world. Of these things I have no doubt.

After Jesus had preached "hard doctrine" at Capernaum, many of his followers were offended "and walked no more with him. Then said Jesus unto the twelve, Will ye also go away?" Simon Peter, the chief Apostle, answered, no doubt for all of his apostolic colleagues—and, for that matter, for all who love the Lord in all ages and know of his absolute necessity and indispensibility in the plan of life and salvation. "Lord," he said, "to whom shall we go? thou hast the words of eternal life, and we believe and are sure that thou art that Christ, the Son of the living God." (John 6:66–69.)

So it was in the first century and so it is now and forevermore: Jesus Christ is the name and the power by which peace and happiness and salvation are to be obtained. On his mighty arm we rely. Because of who he is and what he has done, there is no obstacle to eternal life too great to overcome. Because of him, our minds are at peace. Our souls may rest.

Bibliography

Andrus, Hyrum L. *God, Man and the Universe.* Salt Lake City: Bookcraft, 1968.

Bainton, Roland. *Here I Stand.* New York: Mentor, 1950.

Benson, Ezra Taft. *Come Unto Christ.* Salt Lake City: Deseret Book Co., 1983.

———. *The Teachings of Ezra Taft Benson.* Salt Lake City: Bookcraft, 1988.

Bonhoeffer, Dietrich. *The Cost of Discipleship.* New York: Macmillan, 1963.

Conference Reports of The Church of Jesus Christ of Latter-day Saints. Salt Lake City: The Church of Jesus Christ of Latter-day Saints, October 1969, October 1973, April 1974, October 1985.

Deseret News, 19 December 1914.

Deseret News Weekly, 31 August 1854.

Dummelow, J. R. *The One Volume Bible Commentary.* New York: Macmillan, 1936.

Hafen, Bruce C. "Beauty for Ashes: The Atonement of Jesus Christ." Address given at the Church Educational System Symposium, 12 August 1988, Brigham Young University, Provo, Utah.

Henley, William Ernest. "Invictus."

Hordern, William. *Living by Grace.* Philadelphia: Westminster, 1975.

Hymns of The Church of Jesus Christ of Latter-day Saints. Salt Lake City: The Church of Jesus Christ of Latter-day Saints, 1985.

Journal of Discourses. 26 vols. Liverpool: F. D. Richards & Sons, 1855–86.

Kimball, Spencer W. *The Teachings of Spencer W. Kimball,* ed. Edward L. Kimball. Salt Lake City: Bookcraft, 1980.

Lee, Harold B. *Stand Ye in Holy Places.* Salt Lake City: Deseret Book Co., 1974.

Lewis, C. S. *Mere Christianity.* New York: Macmillan, 1952.

Lund, Gerald N. "Salvation: By Grace or by Works?" *Ensign,* Salt Lake City: The Church of Jesus Christ of Latter-day Saints, April 1981.

Lundwall, N. B., comp. *A Compilation Containing the Lectures on Faith . . . Also a Treatise on True Faith by Orson Pratt. . . .* Salt Lake City: n.d.

MacArthur, John F., Jr. *The Gospel According to Jesus.* Grand Rapids, Michigan: Zondervan, 1988.

MacDonald, George. *George MacDonald: An Anthology,* ed. C. S. Lewis. New York: Macmillan, 1978.

Maxwell, Neal A. *"Not My Will, But Thine."* Salt Lake City: Bookcraft, 1988.

———. *Notwithstanding My Weakness.* Salt Lake City: Deseret Book Co., 1981.

———. *We Will Prove Them Herewith.* Salt Lake City: Deseret Book Co., 1982.

McConkie, Bruce R. *Doctrinal New Testament Commentary.* 3 vols. Salt Lake City: Bookcraft, 1965–73.

———. "Jesus Christ and Him Crucified." *1976 Devotional Speeches of the Year.* Provo, Utah: Brigham Young University Press, 1977.

———. *Mormon Doctrine.* 2nd ed. Salt Lake City: Bookcraft, 1966.

————. *A New Witness for the Articles of Faith*. Salt Lake City: Deseret Book Co., 1985.

————. "The Probationary Test of Mortality." Address to the institute of religion students, University of Utah, 10 January 1982.

————. *The Promised Messiah*. Salt Lake City: Deseret Book Co., 1978.

————. "What Think Ye of Salvation by Grace?" *1983-84 Fireside and Devotional Speeches*. Provo, Utah: Brigham Young University Press, 1984.

McConkie, Joseph F., and Robert L. Millet. *Doctrinal Commentary on the Book of Mormon*. 4 vols. Salt Lake City: Bookcraft, 1987-.

Melvin J. Ballard: Crusader for Righteousness. Salt Lake City: Bookcraft, 1966.

Millet, Robert L., and Joseph F. McConkie. *In His Holy Name*. Salt Lake City: Bookcraft, 1988.

————. *The Life Beyond*. Salt Lake City: Bookcraft, 1986.

Millet, Robert L., and Larry E. Dahl, eds. *The Capstone of Our Religion*. Salt Lake City: Bookcraft, 1989.

Morris, Leon. *The Gospel According to John*. William B. Eerdmans Publishing Co., 1971.

Oaks, Dallin H. *Pure in Heart*. Salt Lake City: Bookcraft, 1988.

Pearson, Glenn L. *Know Your Religion*. Salt Lake City: Bookcraft, 1961.

Pratt, Orson. "The Holy Spirit" [pamphlet]. Liverpool, 1852.

Smith, Joseph. *The Personal Writings of Joseph Smith*, ed. Dean C. Jessee. Salt Lake City: Deseret Book Co., 1984.

————. *Teachings of the Prophet Joseph Smith*, comp. Joseph Fielding Smith. Salt Lake City: Deseret Book Co., 1976.

Smith, Joseph Fielding. *Doctrines of Salvation*, comp. Bruce R. McConkie. 3 vols. Salt Lake City: Bookcraft, 1954-56.

Sperry, Sidney B. *Paul's Life and Letters*. Salt Lake City: Bookcraft, 1955.

Tillich, Paul. *Systematic Theology*. 3 vols. Chicago: University of Chicago Press, 1951-63.

Whitney, Orson F. "The Soul's Captain" in *Improvement Era*. Salt Lake City: The Church of Jesus Christ of Latter-day Saints, April 1926.

Woodward, Kenneth L. "What Mormons Believe." *News-week*, 1 September 1980.
Young Woman's Journal, June 1907.

Subject Index

Scripture Index

OLD TESTAMENT

NEW TESTAMENT

BOOK OF MORMON